Life

After

PIZZA

◆ ◆ ◆ ◆ ◆ ◆

A Cookbook For The
◆ Fast Food Crowd ◆

Great American Opportunities, Inc./Favorite Recipes Press

President: Thomas F. McDow III
Director of Marketing: Roger Conner
Marketing Services Manager: Karen Bird

Editorial Manager: Mary Jane Blount
Editors: Georgia Brazil, Mary Cummings, Jane Hinshaw,
          Linda Jones, Mary Wilson
Typography: William Maul, Sharon Whitehurst

Copyright© 1988 by
Great American Opportunities, Inc.
  P.O. Box 305142
  Nashville, TN 37230

Library of Congress Catalog Number: 88-11018

ISBN: 0-87197-234-4

Manufactured in the United States of America

First Printing 1988   78,100 copies
Second Printing 1993   25,000 copies

Contents

In The Beginning

There is life after pizza, you know. Some hunger crises can't be solved by searching the Yellow Pages for free delivery. Sometimes, in spite of everything, you **have** to—or **want** to cook.

Is someone you want to impress coming to dinner—the minister, your mother or mother-in-law, the Governor, the gang, Tom Cruise or Whitney Houston? *Life After Pizza* can help.

Is it your turn to take a pot to the potluck, look after a sick friend, furnish snacks for "the meeting," take your specialty to the party or furnish something besides the napkins? *Life After Pizza* has the answer.

Do you need the perfect gift—a birthday cake, Christmas candy, edible Valentine, Easter goodies, graduation cookies, Mother's Day breakfast in bed? You can count on *Life After Pizza*.

Do you need a fast food fix and have no wheels? See "Life in the Fast Lane." Are you famished and have the budget of a starving artist? See "Tips from Dagwood." Are you snowbound and stuck with a 'what-you-see-is-what-you-get' cupboard? *Life After Pizza* is full of recipes using ingredients you can always have on hand. Have you run out of money but not out of month? *Life After Pizza* has your number with lots of recipes that don't cost megabucks to taste good.

Whether boiling an egg is a challenge or you're ready to tackle a soufflé, help is on the way. From a grilled cheese sandwich to homemade bread—and all points in between—you'll find just what you want in *Life After Pizza*. And for those times when it's your turn to produce dinner under difficult circumstances, we've provided a selection of menus to get you started and shopping tips to make life easier.

LIFE-SAVING MENUS

See index for recipes.

THE BRUNCH BUNCH
*"Some People Do Cook
    Before Noon"*

Grapefruit Halves
Mushroom Omelets*
Cinnamon-Raisin Biscuits *

COUCH POTATO SUPPER
"Just You and the TV"

Grilled Cheese Sandwich *
Fast Fries *
Super Shake *

CASH-FLOW SPECIAL
"When Money Is the Object"

Porcupines *
Coleslaw *
Sautéed Squash *
Unbelievably Easy
   Peanut Butter Cookies *

THE GANG'S ALL HERE
"Feeding the Hungry Hoards"

Puppy Dogs *
Teenzzi Pizzas *
Easy Dip for Vegetables *
Party Mix *
Velveeta Fudge *

PANIC BUTTON SUPPER
*"Guess Who's Coming
    to Dinner"*

Chicken Tetrazzini *
Tossed Salad with
   Lemon-Herb Dressing *
Italian Bread
Parfaits *

SHOW-OFF DINNER
*"Putting Your Best
   Foot Forward"*

Spinach Dip in a bread bowl *
Stir-Fried Pepper Steak *
Ambrosia Salad *
Easy Party Rice *
Baked Alaska *

MAXING OUT AT THE SUPERMARKET

If you want to eat, you may have to shop. Instead of a boring trip up and down all the aisles, shop in the specialty areas of your market. Make a menu (or use ours for a start) for the day or week, and complete your shopping list from the recipes for each dish. Group the items on your list according to their location in the store and hit the carts running. You'll be through in no time and less likely to forget those essential eggs for the omelet. Here are our suggestions for your next expedition to the supermarket.

THE SALAD BAR

This new section is where you can pick up small amounts of lots of vegetables and fixings, all for a single price per pound. The secret is to go for light weight, expensive items like mushrooms, snow peas or cauliflowerets and to avoid heavier, cheaper foods like carrots, celery and cabbage. Use your stop here for add-ins, stir-fried dishes, perk-ups for humdrum salads or to save the expense of large purchases when you need small amounts.

THE DELI

You can eat for a week and hardly see the stove if you make smart purchases here. Check out the fully cooked lean meats, roasted chickens, barbecue, muffins and bagels, prepared salads and even cheesecake. You can save waste, fuss, time and money.

6

THE DAIRY SHOP

Pick up all your eggs, milk, cheese, yogurt and sour cream here but also watch for the fresh tortillas, biscuits, rolls of cookie dough, refrigerated pie pastry, dips and flavored cream cheese. You'll never go hungry if you keep these foods on hand.

THE FROZEN FOOD CASE

Not only are there terrific frozen dishes and dinners in these cases, but almost every edible imaginable comes ready to thaw, heat and eat. Look for waffles, pancakes, French toast, hashed browns, chicken breast filets, vegetable and pasta combos, frozen bread dough, cakes and mixed fruits and juices. Pick up pie shells, whipped topping and lemonade for a pie or ice cream for easy desserts. If you only have five minutes to shop, this is the aisle to visit.

THE EXPRESS LANE

No matter where you shop in the grocery, checking out is the trick, and using the 12-item express lane is the answer. But which 12 items? Use our list and recipe ideas for a whole week of dinners from a mere dozen purchases. Of course, we suppose you might have a few things on hand. The secret is to buy one large package—3 pounds of ground beef in a single package is still only 1 item.

GROCERY LIST

Family pack of chicken breasts	Large bag shredded cabbage
3 to 5-pound package ground beef	Large package tossed salad
	2-loaf package French bread
Large jar of spaghetti sauce	5-pound bag apples
2-pound package pasta	16-ounce package cheese
1½-dozen carton of eggs	Large box Bisquick
	1 gallon milk

RECIPES FROM THE EXPRESS LANE *

Main Dishes—Spaghetti with Beefed-up, Spaghetti Sauce, Creamed Chicken over Spaghetti, Meat Loaf, Cheese Omelet, Oven-Fried Chicken, Classic Cheese Soufflé, Toad in a Hole, One-Step Baked Spaghetti, Hamburger Pancakes and Chicken and Dumplings.

Main Dishes—Meat Loaf Sandwiches, Sloppy Joes, Club Sandwich, French Toast and Meatball Wedge.

Salads—Coleslaw, Tossed Salad, Waldorf Salad and Stuffed Deviled Eggs.

Breads—French Bread, Mayonnaise Biscuits and Cheesy French Loaf.

Desserts—Apple Crisp, Velvet Crumb Cake (see Bisquick package) and Apples and Cheese.

* See Index for individual recipes.

Thingamajigs

Whether the kitchen shelves and drawers are full of equipment or are bare and you're starting from scratch, identifying what you need and how to use it is essential. Many things look similar—but aren't. A bundt and tube pan may be used for almost the same things except—**never** use a bundt pan for an angel food cake. Blenders and food processors are close cousins. However, food processors can whip cream or knead and mix some doughs—tasks you should never try in the blender. Some utensils have multiple uses. A pancake turner will turn pancakes, remove cookies from cookie sheets and even serve a neat square of cake from a cake pan. A rubber spatula will scoop the last dab of mayonnaise from a jar, scrape the mixer bowl so clean it may not need washing and in a pinch spread frosting on a cake. Other utensils may look like nothing you have ever seen before. However, once you use a wire whisk to blend sauces or a pastry blender to cut the shortening into flour, you'll see how easy it is when you have the "right stuff." The following illustrations may be helpful.

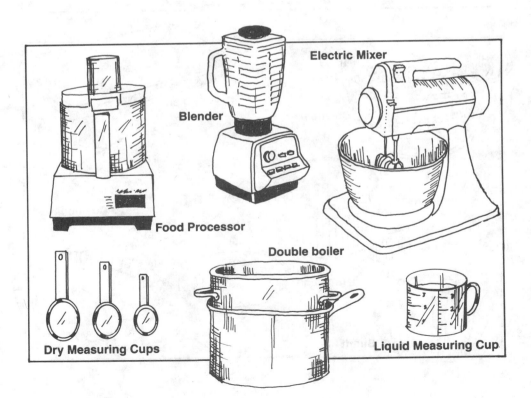

Electric Mixer

Blender

Food Processor

Double boiler

Dry Measuring Cups

Liquid Measuring Cup

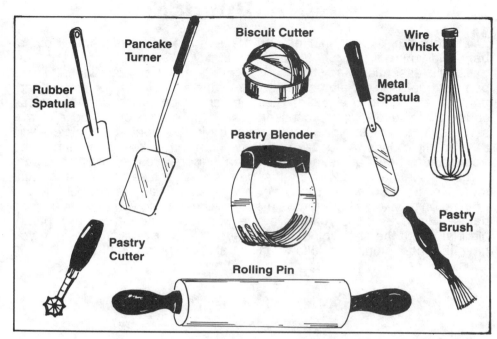

Rubber Spatula

Pancake Turner

Biscuit Cutter

Wire Whisk

Metal Spatula

Pastry Blender

Pastry Cutter

Pastry Brush

Rolling Pin

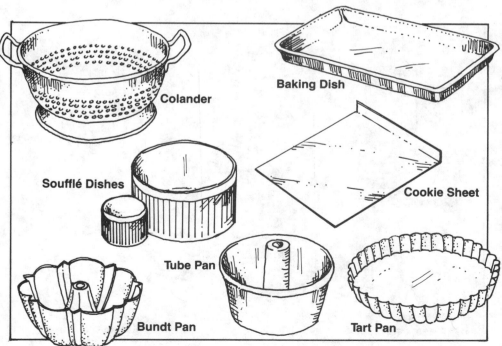

Colander

Baking Dish

Soufflé Dishes

Cookie Sheet

Tube Pan

Bundt Pan

Tart Pan

Food
In The
Fast Lane

♦ ♦ ♦ ♦ ♦ ♦ ♦ ♦ ♦ ♦ ♦ ♦

♦ Eating Out At Home ♦

BURGER HEAVEN

BEST BURGERS

See page 88 for directions for ground beef patties. Pat out thick or thin, giant or tiny, depending on your favorite carry-out. Pan-fry or grill as on page 89. Top with a special sauce; serve on appropriate bun.

Special Sauce—Use bottled or homemade Thousand Island Salad Dressing (page 61) omitting the egg.

What-a-Sauce—Mix 1 tablespoon catsup with 1 tablespoon pickle relish.

Triple Buns—Cut unsliced deli buns into 3 layers, or trim crusts from top and bottom of sliced bun. Use as middle layers of 2 other buns.

FAST FRIES

Prepare frozen French fries or onion rings using package directions. Sprinkle with salt, garlic salt, seasoned salt, Cajun seasoning or taco seasoning.

SUPER SHAKES

Combine 4 scoops ice cream, 2 tablespoons chocolate or strawberry syrup and ¼ cup milk in blender container. Blend on High until thick and creamy. Add 1 or 2 ice cubes and blend until icy for a "frosty" drink.

CHICKEN ON THE WING

For chicken as good as the Colonel's, use our Oven-Fried Chicken (page 99) or make our special seasoning mix for the real thing. Try boned chicken filets for sandwiches or nuggets for dipping.

KENTUCKY-STYLE CHICKEN COATING MIX

3 cups self-rising flour
2 (1-serving) envelopes
   instant tomato soup mix

2 (1½-ounce) packages
   Italian salad dressing mix
1 teaspoon salt

▶ Combine all ingredients in plastic bag; shake to mix. Use as needed.

COLONEL'S BEST CHICKEN

6 chicken pieces
½ cup Coating Mix

1 tablespoon oil
1 tablespoon water

▶ Preheat oven to 350 degrees. Rinse chicken pieces with cold water.
▶ Coat with Kentucky-Style Coating Mix. Coat twice for crispy chicken.
▶ Place in baking pan. Bake for 1 hour or until tender. Brush with mixture of oil and water several times during baking.

CREAM GRAVY

Stir 2 tablespoons flour into chicken pan drippings. Add 1 cup water or milk; mix well. Place on burner on top of stove. Cook over low heat until thickened, stirring constantly. Use this technique for sausage gravy also.

DIPPING SAUCES

Bottled dipping sauce
Catalina salad dressing
Ranch salad dressing
Sweet and sour sauce
Honey and mustard

Chip dips
Honey and barbecue
   sauce
Cheese Sauce
   (pages 12 and 71)

BUFFALO WINGS

3 pounds chicken wings
1 cup packed brown sugar
¼ cup water

1 tablespoon soy sauce
½ cup vinegar
¼ cup catsup

▶ Cut chicken wings into 3 pieces, discarding tip portions. Prepare as for Basic Oven-Fried Chicken (page 99). Bake at 400 degrees for 20 minutes or until brown and crispy.
▶ Combine brown sugar, water, soy sauce, vinegar, catsup and salt in bowl; mix well. Pour over chicken. Bake for 20 minutes longer.
▶ Yields 6 to 8 servings.

MEXICAN FIESTA

Most Mexican fast food involves many of the same basic ingredients, just arranged in different ways. You will need tortillas, meat sauce, cheese sauce, salsa and guacamole.

START WITH THE TORTILLAS

There are flour tortillas and corn tortillas. Each can be served soft or crisp. Tortillas can be found in the dairy section and frozen food section in the market. There is also a light and crispy flour tortilla available in the dairy section. Follow package directions for cooking or heating all of these. Ready-to-fill taco shells and taco chips are on the shelves.

ADD THE MEAT SAUCE

Taco Meat Sauce—Prepare a Basic Ground Beef Scramble (page 92), and add a package of taco seasoning mix, following package directions.

Chili Meat Sauce—Prepare chili (page 93).

POUR ON THE CHEESE SAUCE

Easy—Melt 1 pound Velveeta cheese with 1 can Ro-Tel tomatoes and green chilies in saucepan over medium heat, mixing well.

Easier—Buy plain or jalapeño Cheez Whiz, and microwave or heat until warm and melted.

Easiest—Buy canned mild or hot cheese sauce in the Mexican food section or deli, and warm according to directions.

TOP WITH SALSA AND GUACAMOLE

Salsa—Combine 1 16-ounce can stewed tomatoes, 4 jalapeño peppers, 1 small onion, 1 small tomato, ½ green pepper, salt and pepper in food processor and pulse until chunky.

Guacamole—Combine 1 chopped tomato, ½ cup chopped onion, 2 mashed avocados and 1 tablespoon lemon juice in bowl; mix well. Season with Tabasco sauce, garlic powder, salt and pepper to taste.

TACOS

Fill crisp taco shells with meat sauce, chopped lettuce and tomato, shredded cheese, sour cream and salsa.

BURRITOS

▶ Fill flour tortilla with canned refried beans and/or meat sauce; roll to enclose the filling.
▶ Place in baking dish; drizzle with cheese sauce. Warm in oven.
▶ Garnish with chopped tomato and lettuce. Serve with guacamole, salsa or sour cream.

MEXICAN PIZZA

▶ Place 2 light and crispy flour tortillas on baking sheet rather than on salad shell forms. Bake according to package directions.
▶ Place 1 on serving plate. Spread with refried beans thinned with a small amount of salsa.
▶ Spread a layer of meat sauce on beans. Top with remaining tortilla, chopped tomato and shredded Monterey Jack and Cheddar cheeses.
▶ Broil until cheeses melt.

TACO SALAD

▶ Bake light and crispy flour tortilla salad shells on forms according to package directions or place layer of taco chips on plate. Fill shells or top chips with green salad.
▶ Top salad with avocado wedges, meat sauce (page 12), sour cream and salsa (page 12).

MEXICAN STACK-UP DINNER

▶ Place crushed corn chips, cooked rice, meat sauce (page 12), cheese sauce (page 12), chopped tomatoes, shredded lettuce, chopped onions and salsa (page 12) in separate serving dishes.
▶ Let guests layer their plates in order listed.

CINNAMON CRISPAS

▶ Place light and crispy flour tortillas on baking sheets rather than on salad shell forms. Cut each into 6 wedges.
▶ Bake according to package directions. Coat immediately with mixture of cinnamon and sugar.

PIZZARIA

Piz·za—a large open pie made of a thinly rolled bread dough or other breadlike base, spread with a spice sauce, topped with cheese and an assortment of meats, vegetables and other goodies and then baked or broiled until cheese melts.

START WITH THE DOUGH

Packaged pizza dough mix
Refrigerator pizza dough
Frozen pizza dough rounds
Refrigerator crescent rolls
English muffins

Split French loaves
Frozen bread dough
Flour tortillas
Hot roll mix
Bagels

THEN THE SAUCE AND TOPPINGS

Canned pizza sauce
Canned tomato sauce
Spaghetti Sauce
 (page 106)
Ground Beef Scramble
 (page 92)
Cooked sausage
Pepperoni slices
Mushrooms
Onions
Green peppers
Black olives
Green olives

Italian seasoning
Dried hot red peppers
Canadian bacon
Ham
Pineapple tidbits
Capers
Jalapeño peppers
Red peppers
Anchovies
Parmesan cheese
Romano cheese
Mozzarella cheese
Miniature meatballs

▶ Follow package directions for prepared doughs and mixes.
▶ Broil muffins and French loaves until cheese is melted.

VARIATIONS

Deep-dish Pizza—Place pizza dough in 9-inch pie plate and fill with as many items as desired.

Double-crust Pizza—Place second layer of dough on top of deep-dish pizza and seal edges.

Calzone—Place filling on half the dough and fold over, sealing edges, or prepare Pepperoni Bread (page 119) and double the filling.

Tex-Mex Pizza—Spread dough with refried beans and chili (page 93) and sprinkle with Monterey Jack cheese.

MEAL-A-PEEL

Baked potatoes are the best fast food. Microwave on High (700 to 800 watts) for about 4 minutes for 1 potato (using manufacturer's directions) or bake as on page 78. Fill with yummy toppings for a whole meal with the potato as a dish. Serve for a party with the toppings in dishes for guests to help themselves.

POTATO TOPPINGS

Cheese Sauce
  (pages 12 and 71)
Any chopped vegetable
Ground Beef Scramble
  (page 92)
Chili (page 93)
Cottage cheese
Sour cream
Chives

Creamed Chicken
  (page 101)
Beef Stroganoff (page 94)
Bacon bits
Shredded cheese
Canned onion rings
Meatballs
Spaghetti sauce
Yogurt

DRIVE-IN DELI

Great big sandwiches—for big appetites or for sharing—are put together from the "deli" section of your refrigerator.

SLIM JIMS

Layer Swiss cheese, boiled ham, Secret Sauce (see Special Sauce, page 10), lettuce and tomato on grilled Italian bread.

PHILLY BEEF AND CHEESE

Layer Swiss or Cheddar cheese, roast beef and sautéed onions, mushrooms and green peppers on grilled sesame bun.

MEATBALL WEDGE

Split ½ loaf Italian bread. Scoop out part of the soft bread on bottom half and fill with meatballs (pages 90-91) and spaghetti sauce (page 106).

CONEY DOG

Serve cooked hot dog on bun with Homemade Spaghetti Sauce (page 106).

BRUNCH MUNCHIES

Nearly every fast-food restaurant now opens early in the morning to serve delicious eye-openers for people on the run. Make your own at home to take with you wherever you go—even if you are going back to bed.

BREAKFAST SANDWICHES

Mom's McMuffin—Layer 1 slice Canadian bacon or ham on half a toasted English muffin. Place 1 fried or scrambled egg and 1 slice American cheese on remaining muffin half. Broil until cheese melts. Place halves together.

Breakfast Biscuits—Prepare cut-out biscuits (page 116). Cut out with 3-inch biscuit cutter and bake. Fill with your choice of bacon, ham, sausage, eggs and/or cheese.

Breakfast Bagels or Croissants— Prepare as for Breakfast Biscuits using toasted bagels or hot croissants.

French Toast—Season scrambled egg mixture (page 31) with 1 tablespoon sugar and 1 teaspoon vanilla. Dip bread slices in mixture to coat. Pan-fry in butter in skillet until golden brown. Serve with confectioners' sugar or choice of syrups.

PANCAKES AND SUCH

Use pancake mix prepared according to package directions or frozen pancakes or waffles heated using package directions.

Dollar Pancakes—Drop batter by tablespoonfuls onto hot griddle. Cook until bubbles appear on surface. Turn and cook until brown.

Blueberry Pancakes—Drop several frozen blueberries into pancakes after spooning onto hot griddle. Blueberries cook as pancakes do. Serve with heated blueberry syrup or topping.

Pecan Pancakes—Stir ½ cup chopped pecans into batter. Serve with heated syrup mixed with additional chopped pecans.

Belgian Waffles—Top baked waffles with ice cream or whipped topping and thawed frozen strawberries in syrup.

Cinnamon-Raisin Biscuits—Prepare dough for cut-out biscuits (page 117). Roll into rectangle ¼ inch thick. Sprinkle with mixture of ½ cup sugar and 1 tablespoon cinnamon. Roll as for jelly roll. Cut into slices. Bake as in recipe. Drizzle with glaze (page 125).

HASHED BROWNS

Scattered—Pan-fry frozen hashed brown potatoes in butter or oil in skillet until brown and crispy, stirring frequently.

Smothered—Prepare hashed brown potatoes as above adding chopped onion to taste before cooking.

Covered—Place sliced cheese on hashed brown potatoes after cooking. Cover. Cook for 1 minute or until cheese melts.

ORIENT EXPRESS

Chinese dinners are a great way to make use of whatever happens to be in the refrigerator. Start with one of the packaged or frozen rice dishes and add your own stir-fried fresh vegetables, chicken, pork, shrimp or even fruit. Fried rice, frozen egg rolls, fortune cookies and fruit sherbet complete the menu.

HAM FRIED RICE

½ cup chopped onion
½ cup chopped green pepper
1 clove of garlic, minced
2 tablespoons oil

1 cup grated carrots
1 cup cooked rice
2 eggs, beaten
1 cup chopped cooked ham

▶ Sauté onion, green pepper and garlic in oil in skillet for 5 minutes or until tender. Add carrots and rice. Cook for a minute, stirring constantly.
▶ Stir in eggs. Cook until eggs are set, stirring frequently. Add ham.
▶ Yields 4 servings.

FORTUNE COOKIES

3 egg whites (from
    extra-large eggs)
¾ cup sugar
½ cup (1 stick) melted butter

¼ teaspoon vanilla extract
1 cup unbleached flour
2 tablespoons strong cold tea
Fortunes on paper slips

▶ Preheat oven to 350 degrees. Grease cookie sheet.
▶ Beat egg whites until frothy. Add sugar; mix well.
▶ Add butter, vanilla, flour and tea in order listed, mixing well.
▶ Chill in refrigerator for 30 minutes.
▶ Make 2 cookies at a time. Spoon 2 measuring teaspoons batter for each cookie onto cookie sheet. Spread into 3-inch circle.
▶ Bake for 5 minutes or until brown on bottom and around edges. Remove to wire rack with spatula immediately.
▶ Place fortune on hot cookie; fold in half. Shape into crescent. Cool.
▶ Yields 2 dozen.

YUMMIE NUMMIES

Sometimes all you need is a quick fix for your sweet tooth, and you need to go no further than your refrigerator and this book to recreate your favorites.

HOT CHOCOLATE FUDGE CAKE

▶ Start with a square of Crazy Cake (page 128). Split cake into 2 layers.
▶ Spread 1 scoop ice cream between layers. Top with hot fudge sauce, whipped topping and a maraschino cherry.

PEANUT BUSTER PARFAIT

Make parfait (page 146) using layers of soft ice cream or ice milk, hot fudge sauce and peanuts.

BLIZZARD

Make Super Shakes (page 10) adding ½ cup chopped candy bars, Oreos, nuts, granola or whatever you love.

FUNNEL CAKES

▶ Mix 2 cups Bisquick, 2 cups milk and 2 eggs in bowl.
▶ Heat 1 inch oil in skillet or saucepan over medium-high heat.
▶ Pour batter into funnel holding finger over end.
▶ Drizzle in spiral shape into oil. Cook until brown on both sides.
▶ Drain on paper towel. Coat with confectioners' sugar.

TURNOVERS

▶ Use refrigerator crescent roll dough or frozen puff pastry. Separate rolls into 4 rectangles or cut thawed pastry into squares.
▶ Spoon canned pie filling onto each square; fold dough into triangles, sealing edges. Bake using package directions.

DOUGHNUTS AND DOUGHNUT HOLES

▶ Use refrigerator biscuits. Cut hole in center of each biscuit.
▶ Deep-fry in 365-degree oil until brown. Drain on paper towel.
▶ Shake in bag of ½ cup sugar mixed with 1 tablespoon cinnamon while doughnut is still hot.

The Great Outdoors

Grilling

Cooking outdoors with friends and family is fun and easy. The preparation is done ahead of time, and the clean-up is a breeze. So everyone, including you, can enjoy the good food and have a good time.

"Cooking out" like so many other things means different things to different people. Basically, it means to cook on an open fire or a bed of coals. Barbecue, however, can be the same as "cooking out" or might mean grilled meat which is shredded or sliced to serve. Out West barbecue means beef, and the "particular cut" is usually beef brisket. In the South and East, it usually means pork.

Meats cooked over an open fire are always delicious but taste even better when marinated before cooking or when served with special sauces (see page 85). These sauces are of two basic kinds—the vinegar-based, used to tenderize meats, and the tomato-based. Most commercial barbecue sauces are tomato based and many are excellent—there is a large selection for you to choose from. For interesting change try the various salad dressings available. Italian, Catalina or Sweet and Sour dressings give a different taste treat for marinating meats or for basting sauces.

Don't forget that you can actually prepare your entire meal outdoors. Try some of the following recipes for breads, vegetables and desserts to round out your menu—all on the grill.

To end a cookout meal, it's hard to beat a cold watermelon or a make-your-own sundae bar. Even better, put your friends to work on some good old-fashioned homemade ice cream. You pick the flavor.

BASIC TOMATO-BASED BARBECUE SAUCE

1½ cups catsup or chili sauce
¼ cup vinegar
¼ cup minced onion
⅓ cup packed brown sugar
2 tablespoons Worcestershire
  sauce

1 teaspoon dry mustard
Garlic powder to taste
Chili powder to taste
½ teaspoon salt
¼ teaspoon pepper

▶ Combine all ingredients in saucepan; mix well.
▶ Simmer over low heat until onion is tender and flavors are blended, stirring occasionally.
▶ Brush barbecue sauce over meat during grilling.
▶ Serve remaining sauce with meat.
▶ Yields 2 cups.

BASIC VINEGAR-BASED BARBECUE SAUCE

2 tablespoons grated onion
1 clove of garlic, minced
¼ cup oil
¾ cups vinegar
2 tablespoons lemon juice
Hot sauce to taste

2 tablespoons Worcestershire
  sauce
2 teaspoons dry mustard
Black and cayenne pepper
  to taste
1 teaspoon salt

▶ Sauté onion and garlic in oil in saucepan.
▶ Add vinegar, lemon juice, hot sauce, Worcestershire sauce and seasonings; mix well.
▶ Place meat in shallow dish; pour sauce over top.
▶ Marinate in refrigerator for several hours to overnight, turning several times. Brush marinade on meat during grilling.
▶ Yields 1½ cups.

SAUCY DOGS

*This is an easy appetizer. Let guests cook their own on table-top
hibachi for a party ice-breaker.*

12 or more bamboo skewers
1 package hot dogs

24 slices bacon
1 cup barbecue sauce

▶ Soak skewers in water; drain.
▶ Cut hot dogs into bite-sized pieces; wrap each piece in bacon. Thread on skewers, securing ends of bacon.
▶ Place over low coals on grill or hibachi; brush with barbecue sauce.
▶ Grill until bacon is crisp, turning and brushing with sauce.
▶ Yields 4 dozen.

BARBECUED FLANK STEAK

1   1½-pound flank steak

1 recipe Basic Vinegar-Based
Barbecue Sauce (page 21)

▶ Marinate steak in Barbecue Sauce in refrigerator for 4 hours to overnight, turning occasionally. Drain, reserving marinade.
▶ Grill steak over hot coals for 5 to 7 minutes on each side, basting with reserved marinade every minute or two.
▶ Place steak on serving platter. Slice thinly diagonally across the grain.
▶ Yields 4 servings.

Note—May use 1½-inch thick round steak or chuck steak instead of flank. Cook to desired degree of doneness.

FAJITAS

6 tablespoons oil
¼ cup lemon juice
2 cloves of garlic, minced
6 tablespoons Worcestershire
  sauce
1 teaspoon seasoned salt

1 teaspoon pepper
1   3-pound flank steak
2 onions, sliced
2 green peppers,
  cut into strips

▶ Combine oil, lemon juice, garlic, Worcestershire sauce, seasoned salt and pepper in shallow dish; mix well.
▶ Add steak. Marinate in refrigerator for 24 to 48 hours.
▶ Grill steak 4 inches from coals for 10 minutes or to desired degree of doneness. Slice thinly across the grain.
▶ Sauté onions and green peppers in skillet until tender-crisp; add steak, tossing to mix.
▶ Serve immediately with flour tortillas, guacamole and picante sauce.
▶ Yields 6 to 8 servings.

BARBECUED PORK

1   4 to 5-pound pork
  shoulder

2 recipes Basic Vinegar-Based
Barbecue Sauce (page 21)

▶ Place meat thermometer in thickest part of pork; thermometer should not touch bone. Insert in end of roast to permit turning.
▶ Place pork on grill over low coals; brush with Barbecue Sauce.
▶ Grill for 30 to 40 minutes per pound or to 185 degrees on meat thermometer, basting and turning occasionally.
▶ Let stand until cool enough to handle; remove and discard fat and bone.
▶ Pull meat apart; place in baking dish. Rewarm, covered, in 350-degree oven for 20 minutes. Serve with remaining sauce.
▶ Yields 10 servings.

BARBECUED SPARERIBS

Prebaking in the oven prevents spareribs from overbrowning and drying out on grill.

5 pounds spareribs

2 recipes Basic Tomato-Based Barbecue Sauce (page 21)

▶ Preheat oven to 350 degrees.
▶ Place spareribs in foil-lined baking pan.
▶ Bake, uncovered, for 1 hour. Drain.
▶ Brush Barbecue Sauce on spareribs; place on grill over low coals.
▶ Grill for 30 minutes, turning and basting frequently with sauce.
▶ Cut spareribs into 2 or 3-rib portions; serve with remaining sauce.
▶ Yields 6 servings.

GLAZED HAM SLICE

1 center ham slice,
½ inch thick

½ cup whole cranberry sauce
2 tablespoons brown sugar

▶ Make several ½-inch cuts through fat around edge of ham slice; do not cut into meat.
▶ Place on grill 5 inches from hot coals.
▶ Grill for 5 minutes on each side.
▶ Spread top with cranberry sauce; sprinkle with brown sugar.
▶ Grill for 2 minutes longer.
▶ Yields 4 servings.

BARBECUED CHICKEN

1 cup vinegar
⅓ cup oil
1 teaspoon (or more) hot sauce
2 tablespoons Worcestershire sauce

Salt, garlic powder and onion powder to taste
2 broiler chickens, split into halves

▶ Combine vinegar, oil, hot sauce, Worcestershire sauce and seasonings in bowl; mix well.
▶ Place chicken halves on grill over medium coals; brush with sauce.
▶ Grill for 1 hour or until chickens are tender, turning and basting frequently.
▶ Yields 4 to 6 servings.

SHISH KABOBS

Combining different kinds of meats and vegetables to plan a well-balanced good tasting meal is always a challenge. Shish Kabobs take away the struggle and make it all fun.

CREATE YOUR OWN GREAT SHISH KABOBS

Create a meal on a stick with the great combinations possible from the list below. Be even more creative, and add some different combinations of your own. Have fun with an age-old way of grilling.

Meat

Beef cubes and strips
Ground beef meatballs
Veal cubes
Lamb cubes
Pork cubes
Sausages

Seafood

Shrimp
Scallops
Lobster tails
Fish cubes
Oysters wrapped in bacon

Vegetables

Zucchini chunks
Yellow squash slices
Green, red or yellow
   pepper squares
Mushroom caps
Onion wedges
Cherry tomatoes
Boiled new potatoes
Brussels sprouts
Corn ear pieces
Eggplant cubes
Water chestnuts
Boiled carrot chunks

Poultry

Chicken cubes and strips
Turkey cubes and strips
Chicken livers

► Use tender cuts of meat, or allow extra time to marinate meat.
► Cut everything into bite-sized chunks which are not too small.
► Combine ingredients that need the same length of time to cook.
► Add the more tender ingredients on additional skewers toward the end of grilling time.

JUMBO SHRIMP KABOBS

1 cup French salad dressing
¼ cup lemon juice
1 tablespoon chopped
  parsley

18 jumbo shrimp, peeled
6 lemon wedges
12 cherry tomatoes
12 chunks green pepper

▶ Combine French dressing, lemon juice and parsley in bowl; add shrimp.
▶ Marinate in refrigerator for several hours. Drain, reserving marinade.
▶ Place 1 lemon wedge on each of 6 metal skewers.
▶ Alternate shrimp, cherry tomatoes and green pepper on skewers.
▶ Grill over medium coals for 6 minutes, turning once and brushing with reserved marinade.
▶ Yields 6 servings.

VEGETABLE KABOBS

Substitute the vegetables which you prefer.

Bamboo skewers
Zucchini, thickly sliced
Mushrooms

Cherry tomatoes
Pearl onions
Italian salad dressing

▶ Soak bamboo skewers in water for several minutes.
▶ Marinate vegetables in Italian dressing in bowl for several hours. Drain vegetables, reserving marinade. Thread onto skewers. Place on grill over low coals.
▶ Grill for 10 minutes or until vegetables are tender-crisp, turning and basting frequently with reserved marinade.

FRUIT KABOBS

Use your favorite fruit for a light dessert.

8 bamboo skewers
2 large bananas
3 large peaches

16 large strawberries
¼ cup honey
1 tablespoon lemon juice

▶ Soak bamboo skewers in water for several minutes.
▶ Drain skewers. Cut bananas and peaches into chunks. Thread fruits alternately onto skewers.
▶ Mix honey and lemon juice; brush on fruit.
▶ Grill 5 inches from low coals for 5 minutes or until warm and glazed, turning and basting frequently.
▶ Yields 8 servings.

FOILED POTATOES

4 potatoes, peeled, sliced
1 onion, thinly sliced
¼ cup butter, sliced

Salt and pepper to taste
1½ cups shredded Cheddar
    cheese

▶ Layer potatoes, onion, butter and seasonings on large piece of heavy-duty aluminum foil.
▶ Fold foil to enclose vegetables, sealing seam tightly.
▶ Grill over hot coals for 1 hour or until potatoes are tender. Turn foil packet occasionally to cook evenly.
▶ Open foil; sprinkle with cheese.
▶ Let stand on grill until cheese melts.
▶ Yields 4 servings.

GRILLED CORN ON THE COB

6 unhusked ears of corn
6 tablespoons melted butter

Salt to taste

▶ Pull back husks from corn ears; remove silks.
▶ Brush kernels with butter; sprinkle with salt.
▶ Pull husks up to cover corn; wrap in aluminum foil.
▶ Place on grill over hot coals.
▶ Roast for 25 minutes or until tender, turning occasionally.
▶ Remove foil and husks. Serve with additional butter and salt.
▶ Yields 6 servings.

CHEESY FRENCH LOAF

Creole Bread and Zesty French Loaves (page 118) can also be prepared in this manner.

½ cup butter, softened
½ cup Parmesan cheese
¼ teaspoon garlic powder

¼ teaspoon paprika
1 tablespoon sesame seed
1 medium loaf French bread

▶ Combine butter, Parmesan cheese, garlic powder, paprika and sesame seed in bowl; mix well.
▶ Cut bread in half lengthwise; spread cut surfaces with butter.
▶ Place buttered surfaces together; wrap in aluminum foil.
▶ Heat on grill over medium coals until butter is melted. Slice diagonally.
▶ Yields 8 servings.

Eggs-actly Right

Eggs

Take a look at an egg. That didn't take long, you say? If you think of an egg only as something you don't have time to eat at breakfast, you have no idea what a treasure lies in that well-engineered little oval. It is a near perfect convenience food—never out of season and always handy. It is the basis for some of the world's easiest, most versatile and most elegant dishes—suitable for any meal, any hour or any occasion.

Eggs come in various sizes and colors. Most recipes assume you buy large ones. Your grandmother may tell you brown eggs are more nutritious but color makes no difference at all—even in the taste. Just make sure the shell isn't cracked before you use it. It is important to buy fresh eggs because they have a better taste and texture. For some purposes, however, eggs can be too fresh. Do not use eggs fresher than 3 days for boiling, beating and baking.

Important!! Eggs should always be cooked over low heat. High heat causes eggs to become hard or rubbery.

HOW TO BOIL AN EGG

The simplest way to cook an egg is to boil it either hard or soft. The method is the same but soft-boiled eggs do need to be timed.

▶ Place the eggs in a saucepan. Add enough cold water to cover eggs by at least 1 inch. Bring to a boil over high heat. Remove from heat and cover tightly.
▶ Let stand for 2 to 4 minutes for soft-boiled eggs or let stand for 25 minutes for hard-boiled eggs.
▶ Serve soft-boiled eggs warm but try the eggs cooked to slightly different times until you find the way you like them best; 10 or 15 seconds makes a difference.
▶ Run cold water over hard-boiled eggs until they are cool. Shake the pan to crack the shells for quicker cooling and easier peeling. Peel under cold running water and shells will slip off more easily.
▶ Do not crack the shells if the eggs will not be peeled and used until later. Mark them with a pencil so hard-boiled and raw eggs do not become a disastrous case of mistaken identity.

STUFFED DEVILED EGGS

6 hard-boiled eggs
1/4 cup mayonnaise
1 teaspoon vinegar
1/4 teaspoon salt
1/8 teaspoon pepper

▶ Cut eggs into halves lengthwise. Remove yolks gently. Place yolks in small bowl; reserve the whites.
▶ Mash yolks with fork. Add mayonnaise, vinegar, salt and pepper; mix well.
▶ Spoon yolk mixture into egg whites; arrange on plate. Chill in refrigerator.
▶ Yields 12 egg halves.

VARIATIONS

Mexican—Add 3 tablespoons drained and chopped Ro-Tel tomatoes with green chilies. Mix as directed above.

Deviled Ham—Reduce mayonnaise to 2 tablespoons and add one 2¼-ounce can deviled ham and 2 tablespoons ripe chopped olives. Mix as directed above.

Pizza—Reduce mayonnaise to 2 tablespoons and add 2 tablespoons pizza sauce and 1/8 teaspoon garlic powder. Mix as directed above.

Relish—Add 1 teaspoon mustard and 2 tablespoons pickle relish. Mix as directed above.

Shrimp—Add 3 tablespoons chopped cooked shrimp and 1 teaspoon lemon juice. Mix as directed above.

Olive—Add 6 chopped stuffed olives and 2 teaspoons prepared mustard. Mix as directed above.

EVERYTHING ELSE ABOUT EGGS

Everything else you do with eggs—except decorate them for Easter—requires that you break the egg first. It is always a good idea to break each egg into a small bowl and then add it to whatever you are making. In case you happen to get a bad egg, you haven't ruined the whole production.

BAKED EGGS

► Butter a 5 or 6-ounce ovenproof ramekin.
► Break 1 or 2 eggs into the ramekin. Sprinkle eggs with salt and pepper.
► Bake in preheated 325-degree oven for 15 to 20 minutes or until whites are set and yolks are soft.

VARIATIONS

Eggs Mornay—Spoon a small amount of Cheese Sauce (page 71) into ramekin, break eggs into sauce and spoon more sauce over top. Bake as directed above.

Cheesy Eggs—Top eggs in ramekin with 1 tablespoon cream, 1 teaspoon butter and sprinkle with cheese. Bake as directed above.

Party Eggs—Pour 1 tablespoon cream and a small amount of chopped asparagus, mushrooms or chopped ham into ramekin. Add eggs; bake as directed above.

Corned Beef Eggs—Pack ⅓ cup canned corned beef into ramekin or muffin cup. Make a deep indentation in the center big enough for 1 egg. Bake as directed above.

Eggs in Bacon Rings—Line ramekin with strip of partially cooked bacon. Bake as directed above.

Egg Nests—Line ramekin with buttered bread slices. Bake as directed above.

FRIED EGGS

► Place 1 to 3 tablespoons butter in 8-inch skillet. Heat over medium heat until hot enough to sizzle a drop of water; reduce heat.
► Break 1 egg at a time into saucer. Slide gently into skillet.
► For "sunny side up" eggs, cook just until whites are set. For turned eggs, cook until whites are opaque and turn very carefully with egg turner. Cook each until yolks are of desired firmness.

TOAD IN A HOLE

► Cut 1½-inch circle from center of bread slice. Place in butter in skillet.
► Slide egg onto bread, centering yolk in hole.
► Cook until bread is light brown on bottom. Turn bread with egg. Cook to desired firmness. Invert onto serving plate.

SCRAMBLED EGGS

▶ Break 1 or 2 eggs for each serving into bowl.
▶ Add 1 tablespoon milk or cream for each egg and salt and pepper to taste. Beat with wire whisk or fork until well mixed.
▶ Place 1½ teaspoons butter for each egg in skillet. Heat over medium heat until hot enough to sizzle a drop of water.
▶ Add eggs; reduce heat to low. As eggs set on bottom, lift gently with spatula, allowing uncooked egg to flow underneath and turning until eggs are set but not dry.

VARIATIONS

Green Eggs and Ham—Add 1 or 2 drops of blue food coloring and chopped cooked ham. Scramble as directed above.

Entrée—Add crumbled crisp-fried bacon, cooked sausage and chopped ham. Scramble as directed above. Serve in warm pita rounds for a change.

Cheese—Add favorite shredded cheese. Scramble as directed above.

Mexicali Eggs—Add crushed corn chips and chopped green chilies. Scramble as directed above. Serve rolled in warm flour tortillas.

Herb—Add minced chives, parsley, tarragon or chervil. Scramble as directed above.

Mushroom—Add sautéed mushrooms or other fresh vegetables such as green peppers, tomatoes or asparagus. Scramble as directed above.

Marmalade—Add marmalade or your favorite preserves. Scramble as directed above.

Creamy—Cook egg mixture in top of double boiler over simmering water until thick and creamy, stirring occasionally. Scramble as directed above. Serve on English muffins.

DENVER SCRAMBLE

½ cup chopped mushrooms
¼ cup chopped onion
2 tablespoons chopped
   green pepper
¼ cup chopped ham
2 tablespoons butter
8 eggs
⅓ cup milk

▶ Sauté mushrooms, onion, green pepper and ham in butter in skillet until vegetables are tender-crisp.
▶ Beat eggs with milk in bowl. Add to mixture in skillet.
▶ Cook for 5 to 8 minutes or until set but not dry, folding gently with spatula.
▶ Yields 6 servings.

BASIC OMELET

3 eggs
1 tablespoon water
¼ teaspoon salt

⅛ teaspoon pepper
1 tablespoon butter

▶ Combine eggs, water, salt and pepper in bowl; beat with wire whisk until yolks and whites are blended.
▶ Melt butter in 7-inch omelet pan over medium heat, tilting to coat pan. Heat until butter stops foaming. Add eggs.
▶ Cook until bottom is set, shaking pan occasionally to keep omelet moving freely in pan.
▶ Lift edges with spatula to allow uncooked egg to run under omelet. Cook until set and light brown on bottom. Remove from heat.
▶ Lift 1 side of omelet with spatula. Fold omelet in half. Slide onto serving plate. Serve immediately.
▶ Yields 1 main-dish serving.

OMELET FILLINGS

Spread prepared filling on half the omelet just before folding over.

Ham Omelet—Add ¾ cup chopped cooked ham.

Cheese Omelet—Add ½ cup shredded cheese.

Omelet Aux Fines Herbs—Add 4 teaspoons mixed dried herbs or ¼ cup chopped fresh herbs such as parsley, chives, basil, tarragon or thyme.

Mushroom Omelet—Add ½ cup sautéed mushrooms.

Asparagus Omelet—Add ½ cup well-drained cooked asparagus.

OMELET SAUCES

Beef up your omelet by spooning an easy sauce over it.

▶ Start with cream sauce or cheese sauce (pages 12 and 71) or a can of condensed soup heated with ½ soup can milk.
▶ Add chicken, turkey, ham, dried beef, cooked sausage, crumbled crisp-fried bacon, shrimp, scallops or vegetables.

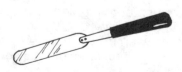

QUICHES

The rumor that real men don't eat quiche was started by a real man who wanted the whole thing for himself. It's a great dish for family, friends or parties and can be concocted to suit any taste.

QUICHE RAMBO

This is really the classic Quiche Lorraine with a new name to protect the sensitivities of real men.

½ pound bacon	1 baked 9-inch pie shell
2 medium onions, chopped	3 eggs
2 cups shredded Swiss cheese	1½ cups half and half
	Salt and pepper to taste

▶ Preheat oven to 350 degrees.
▶ Cook bacon in skillet until crisp; drain on paper towel. Reserve 3 tablespoons drippings. Sauté onions in reserved drippings for 3 to 5 minutes.
▶ Sprinkle cheese in pie shell. Add crumbled bacon and sautéed onions.
▶ Beat eggs, half and half and seasonings in bowl. Pour over layers.
▶ Bake for 35 to 40 minutes or until center is almost firm and top is brown.
▶ Yields 6 servings.

EASY HAM AND CHEESE QUICHE

1 cup shredded Cheddar cheese	½ cup chopped cooked ham
½ cup chopped cooked broccoli	4 eggs, beaten
1 baked 9-inch pie shell	1 10-ounce can Cheddar cheese soup
	½ cup half and half

▶ Preheat oven to 350 degrees.
▶ Layer cheese, broccoli and ham in pie shell. Beat eggs in bowl with soup and half and half. Pour over broccoli.
▶ Bake for 50 minutes or until knife inserted in center comes out clean. Let quiche stand for 5 minutes before serving.
▶ Yield: 6 servings.

VARIATIONS

Bacon-Asparagus Quiche—Use American cheese, crumbled crisp-fried bacon, cooked asparagus and cream of onion soup. Bake as directed above.

Chicken-Mushroom Quiche—Use Monterey Jack cheese, chopped cooked chicken, sliced mushrooms and cream of mushroom soup. Bake as directed above.

Turkey-Spinach Quiche—Use Swiss cheese, chopped cooked turkey, chopped cooked spinach and cream of celery soup. Bake as directed above.

MAKE-AHEAD EGG AND SAUSAGE BAKE

This is an easy main dish for a brunch or supper. Use either mild or hot sausage.

12 slices bread
1 pound pork sausage
2 cups shredded
   Cheddar cheese

6 eggs, beaten
2 cups milk
1 teaspoon salt

▶ Preheat oven to 325 degrees.
▶ Trim bread crusts. Cook sausage in skillet, stirring until brown and crumbly; drain. Layer 6 bread slices, sausage, cheese and remaining bread in 9x13-inch baking dish.
▶ Combine eggs, milk and salt in bowl; beat until smooth. Pour over layers. Cover with foil.
▶ Chill casserole in refrigerator overnight.
▶ Remove aluminum foil. Bake casserole for 1 hour or until brown and set. Cut into squares.
▶ Yields 8 servings.

SEPARATING EGGS

The time has come to talk about separating egg yolks from egg whites and what to do when you've got them separated.

▶ Tap an egg sharply against the edge of a small bowl. Insert thumb nails into cracked shell just enough to separate the shell into halves, allowing the white to fall into the bowl but retaining the yolk in 1 shell half.
▶ Transfer the yolk carefully back and forth from 1 shell half to the other until all the white has fallen into the bowl. Remove any small portions of egg shell with spoon.
▶ Place egg yolk in another bowl. Transfer the egg white to a larger bowl and break remaining eggs, 1 at a time, into small bowl. If the yolk breaks and even a tiny amount becomes mixed with white, reserve that egg for another use. The whites will not beat successfully with *any* yolk in them.

BEATING EGG WHITES

▶ Use a deep narrow-bottomed stainless steel or glass mixer bowl. Do not use a plastic or aluminum bowl. Do not use a blender or food processor. Have egg whites at room temperature and be sure they are free of yolk.
▶ Beat egg whites with electric mixer at low speed until they are foamy. Add ¼ teaspoon cream of tartar and a pinch of salt for every 4 egg whites.

▶ Beat at high speed until egg whites form stiff peaks when mixer is stopped and beaters lifted. Appearance should be glossy. Use egg whites at once as they begin to lose air almost immediately.

▶ When beating egg whites for meringue, add the sugar 1 tablespoon at a time, starting when egg whites begin to form peaks and beating until stiff.

FOLDING IN EGG WHITES

▶ Stiffly beaten egg whites must be added to a batter or sauce quickly and gently to retain as much air as possible. Always fold the egg whites into the heavier mixture.

▶ Stir about ¼ of the egg whites gently into batter. Spoon remaining egg whites on top.

▶ Using a wide rubber spatula, cut down through both mixtures to the bottom of the bowl. Lift batter toward side of bowl and up.

▶ Repeat process, turning bowl a quarter turn with each stroke until mixtures are blended. Do not overmix; process will require about a minute.

EASY SOUPER SOUFFLÉ

Having mastered separating, beating and folding, you now know everything you need to know to try an "elegant but easy" soufflé or puffy omelet. Serve soufflés and puffy omelets immediately.

1 10-ounce can Cheddar cheese soup	1 cup shredded sharp Cheddar cheese
Cayenne pepper to taste	6 eggs, separated

▶ Preheat oven to 300 degrees. Grease bottom of 2-quart casserole or soufflé dish.

▶ Heat soup, cayenne pepper and cheese in saucepan over low heat until cheese melts; stirring constantly. Remove from heat.

▶ Beat egg yolks until thick and lemon-colored. Stir in soup mixture.

▶ Beat egg whites just until stiff glossy peaks form. Fold egg whites gently into soup mixture.

▶ Spoon gently into prepared dish. Make 1-inch deep indentation in a circle in top of mixture 1-inch from side of dish. Bake for 1 hour or until light brown. Serve immediately.

▶ Yields 6 servings.

VARIATIONS

Swiss—Use cream of asparagus soup, Swiss cheese and nutmeg. Bake as directed above.

Ranch—Use tomato soup, Monterey Jack cheese and chili powder. Bake as directed above.

Nordic—Use cream of chicken soup, Jarlsberg cheese and parsley. Bake as directed above.

CLASSIC CHEESE SOUFFLÉ

¼ cup butter
¼ cup flour
1 teaspoon salt
⅛ teaspoon cayenne pepper

1½ cups milk
2 cups shredded Cheddar
   cheese
6 eggs, separated

▶ Preheat oven to 325 degrees. Grease bottom of 2-quart soufflé dish.
▶ Melt butter in saucepan. Stir in flour, salt and cayenne pepper until smooth. Add milk gradually. Cook until thickened, stirring constantly. Stir in cheese until melted. Remove from heat.
▶ Beat egg yolks lightly. Stir a small amount of hot sauce into egg yolks; stir egg yolks slowly into hot sauce.
▶ Beat egg whites just until stiff peaks form. Fold gently into yolk mixture.
▶ Spoon into prepared dish. Make 1-inch indentation in a circle in top of mixture 1 inch from side of dish. Bake for 1 hour or until puffed and golden.
▶ Yields 6 servings.

VARIATIONS

▶ Add 2 cups chopped cooked ham or chicken; 1 cup crumbled bacon; 1 cup chopped cooked asparagus, mushrooms or spinach. Bake as directed above.
▶ Substitute your favorite cheese.

PUFFY OMELET

4 eggs, separated
¼ cup cold water
¼ teaspoon salt

¼ teaspoon cream of tartar
2 tablespoons butter

▶ Preheat oven to 350 degrees.
▶ Beat egg yolks with water and salt until light and fluffy.
▶ Beat egg whites until foamy. Add cream of tartar; beat until stiff glossy peaks form. Fold gently into egg yolks.
▶ Melt butter in heavy ovenproof 10-inch skillet over medium heat. Add egg mixture. Reduce heat. Cook for 3 to 5 minutes or until brown on bottom.
▶ Place skillet in oven. Bake for 10 to 15 minutes or until surface is golden and springs back when lightly touched. Sprinkle with fillings if desired.
▶ Loosen from side of pan with spatula. Fold carefully in half. Invert onto serving plate. Serve immediately.
▶ Yields 2 main-dish servings.

PUFFY DESSERT OMELET

▶ Add 2 tablespoons sugar to egg yolk mixture. Bake as directed above.
▶ Fill baked omelet with sweetened fresh strawberries, peaches, blueberries, bananas or canned pie filling.
▶ Sprinkle with confectioners' sugar; top with whipped cream.

Pigging Out

Snacks

We all know about the most important meal of the day—the one that begins when we get up and ends when we go to bed. Whether we call it snacks, munchies, grazing or the cure for bored teeth, we love every mouthful. The secret to successful pigging out, however, is ease of preparation. The food shouldn't take much longer to fix than to eat!

The following recipes are for quick, no-fuss goodies perfect for a couch-potato evening, hanging out with friends, a quick pick-me-up, gifts for special people, parties, or first aid on a nonstop day. Make your choice—then fix and eat!

HAM AND CHEESE BALL

1 cup shredded Cheddar
  cheese
8 ounces cream cheese,
  softened
1 4-ounce can deviled ham

2 tablespoons finely
  chopped pimento
1 teaspoon minced onion
Chopped parsley

▶ Combine Cheddar cheese and cream cheese in mixer bowl; beat until well mixed.
▶ Add deviled ham, pimento and onion; mix well. Chill for 2 hours.
▶ Shape into ball; roll in parsley. Serve with crackers.
▶ Yields 2½ cups.

BEEFY ROLL-UPS

1 small jar dried beef   8 ounces chive-flavored
cream cheese, softened

▶ Separate slices of dried beef; spread each piece evenly with softened cream cheese.
▶ Roll beef as for jelly roll to enclose filling. Arrange on serving plate.
▶ Serve with toothpicks.
▶ Yields 8 servings.

PUPPY DOGS

2　8-count packages
　hot dogs
2　16-ounce packages bacon

2 cups packed light brown
　sugar
32 small dinner rolls

▶ Cut hot dogs in half crosswise; wrap 1 slice bacon spiral-fashion around each hot dog, securing with toothpicks.
▶ Alternate layers of hot dogs and brown sugar in Crock•Pot.
▶ Cook on Low for 10 to 12 hours or until bacon is brown; drain.
▶ Transfer hot dogs to baking dish; remove toothpicks.
▶ Keep warm in 250-degree oven until serving time.
▶ Serve on dinner rolls.
▶ Yields 32 servings.

TEENZZI PIZZAS

2　10-count cans
　refrigerator biscuits
1　16-ounce jar pizza sauce
2 cups grated mozzarella
　cheese

1　4-ounce package
　sliced pepperoni
½ cup chopped green pepper
½ cup sliced stuffed
　green olives

▶ Preheat oven to 350 degrees.
▶ Place biscuits on foil-lined baking sheet; flatten into 4-inch circles.
▶ Spoon pizza sauce over biscuits; sprinkle with cheese.
▶ Arrange 3 slices pepperoni in triangle on each pizza. Sprinkle with green pepper and olives.
▶ Bake for 10 to 15 minutes or until crust is brown and cheese bubbles.
▶ Yields 20 miniature pizzas.

SAUSAGE AND CHEESE BALLS

You can use either mild or hot sausage.

1 pound sausage, crumbled
3 cups Bisquick

1 pound sharp Cheddar
  cheese, shredded

▶ Preheat oven to 400 degrees. Combine uncooked sausage, Bisquick and cheese in bowl; mix well.
▶ Shape into small balls; place on baking sheet.
▶ Bake for 10 minutes or until brown; drain on paper towels.
▶ Yields 3 dozen sausage balls.

MICROWAVE NACHO QUICKIE

1   7-ounce bag tortilla chips
1   16-ounce can chili
    without beans

2 cups shredded Monterey
  Jack cheese with jalapeño
  peppers

▶ Layer chips, chili and cheese on serving plate.
▶ Microwave on High for 1 minute or until cheese is melted.
▶ Yields 6 servings.

PEANUT BUTTER STICKS

1   1-pound loaf bread
2 cups peanut butter

1 cup (about) oil

▶ Preheat oven to 250 degrees. Trim crusts from bread. Cut each bread slice into finger-sized strips. Place strips and trimmings on baking sheet.
▶ Toast until very dry and light brown; crush trimmings to make fine crumbs.
▶ Blend peanut butter with enough oil in bowl to make a thick liquid.
▶ Dip toasted strips into peanut butter; roll in crumbs, coating well.
▶ Place on waxed paper. Let stand for 12 to 24 hours or until dry.
▶ Yields 5 dozen.

GRAN-BANAN-OLA

2 tablespoons (or more) milk
¼ cup honey

½ cup granola
3 bananas, thickly sliced

▶ Blend milk and honey in bowl; place granola in plastic bag.
▶ Dip bananas into honey mixture; shake in granola, coating well.
▶ Serve on toothpicks.
▶ Yields 4 to 6 servings.

GRANOLA

2½ cups oats
1 cup coconut
½ cup chopped almonds
½ cup sesame seed
½ cup sunflower seed

½ cup wheat germ
½ cup honey
¼ cup oil
½ cup chopped dried apricots
½ cup raisins

▶ Preheat oven to 300 degrees.
▶ Mix oats, coconut, almonds, sesame seed, sunflower seed and wheat germ in 9x13-inch baking pan.
▶ Mix honey and oil in bowl. Pour over oats mixture; mix well.
▶ Bake for 45 minutes, stirring every 15 minutes.
▶ Stir in apricots and raisins. Cool. Store in airtight container.
▶ Yields 6½ cups.

CRUNCHY MUNCHY MIX

2 cups Quaker Corn Bran
2 cups Honey Graham Oh's
2 cups Captain Crunch
1 cup quick-cooking oats
2 cups broken pecans

¾ teaspoon cinnamon
¼ teaspoon salt
½ cup (1 stick) butter
⅓ cup honey
¼ cup packed brown sugar

▶ Preheat oven to 325 degrees.
▶ Mix cereals, oats, pecans, cinnamon and salt in large bowl.
▶ Combine butter, honey and brown sugar in sauceapan. Heat until well mixed, stirring constantly. Pour over cereal; mix well.
▶ Spread in buttered 10x15-inch pan. Bake for 30 minutes; stir frequently.
▶ Spoon onto waxed paper immediately, stirring and breaking apart as mix cools. Store in airtight container.
▶ Yields 8 cups.

CARAMEL CRUNCHIES

¼ cup (½ stick) margarine
28 caramels
2 tablespoons milk

3½ cups cornflakes
½ cup chopped nuts
½ cup coconut (optional)

▶ Combine margarine, caramels and milk in large saucepan.
▶ Cook over low heat until caramels are melted, mixing well; remove from heat. Add cornflakes, nuts and coconut; mix well.
▶ Drop by tablespoonfuls onto waxed paper. Cool.
▶ Yields 2 dozen.

RANCH CRACKERS

1 cup oil
1 envelope dry ranch salad
   dressing mix
½ teaspoon garlic powder

¼ teaspoon dill
½ teaspoon lemon pepper
1   16-ounce box oyster
   crackers

▶ Combine oil, dressing mix and seasonings in bowl; mix well.
▶ Let stand for 1 hour.
▶ Place crackers in container with tight fitting lid.
▶ Pour oil mixture over crackers; shake well.
▶ Let stand for 24 hours, shaking occasionally.
▶ Store in airtight container.
▶ Yields 6 cups.

NIBBLES AND BITS

2 cups milk chocolate chips
1 cup peanut butter
1   12-ounce package
   Crispix cereal

2 cups confectioners' sugar

▶ Melt chocolate chips with peanut butter in large saucepan over low heat, stirring constantly.
▶ Add cereal; stir gently until cereal is well coated.
▶ Place half the confectioners' sugar in large paper bag.
▶ Add cereal mixture and remaining confectioners' sugar; shake until cereal is coated.
▶ Spread in single layer on waxed paper. Cool.
▶ Yields 10 cups.

PARTY MIX

¾ cup dry roasted peanuts
1 cup broken pretzels
10 cups Crispix or mixed
   Chex cereals
2 cups Honey Graham Chex

½ cup (1 stick) margarine
2 tablespoons Worcestershire
   sauce
2½ teaspoons seasoned salt

▶ Preheat oven to 225 degrees.
▶ Mix peanuts, pretzels and cereals in 9x13-inch baking dish.
▶ Combine margarine, Worcestershire sauce and seasoned salt in small saucepan. Heat over low heat until margarine is melted; mix well.
▶ Pour over cereal mixture; toss to mix well.
▶ Bake for 1½ hours, stirring every 20 minutes. Cool.
▶ Store in airtight container.
▶ Yields 12 cups.

VELVEETA FUDGE

Don't tell what's in this fudge until your friends beg for more.

1 cup (2 sticks) butter
8 ounces Velveeta cheese, chopped
1½ teaspoons vanilla extract

2   16-ounce packages confectioners' sugar
½ cup cocoa
Chopped pecans (optional)

▶ Melt butter and cheese in saucepan over low heat, stirring constantly; mix in vanilla.
▶ Pour over mixture of confectioners' sugar and cocoa in bowl; mix quickly until smooth.
▶ Spread in buttered 9x13-inch dish; pat pecans over top. Let stand until set; cut into squares.
▶ Yields 3 pounds.

WHITE CHOCOLATE BARK

1 pound white chocolate, broken

1 cup broken pecans
1 cup broken pretzels

▶ Melt chocolate over hot water in double boiler, stirring constantly.
▶ Stir in pecans and pretzels.
▶ Pour into buttered 9x13-inch dish. Chill until firm.
▶ Break into pieces.
▶ Yields 1¼ pounds.

CRISPY TREATS

40 marshmallows
½ cup (1 stick) margarine

6 cups crisp rice cereal

▶ Melt marshmallows and margarine in saucepan over low heat, stirring constantly. Pour over cereal in bowl, tossing to mix well.
▶ Pack into buttered 9x13-inch dish. Cool until firm. Cut into squares.
▶ Yields 6 dozen.

VARIATION
Add chocolate chips, chopped nuts, gumdrops or green and red candied cherries. Substitute other cereals for crisp rice cereal. Drop by spoonfuls onto waxed paper if preferred.

GUMMY BERRIES

1 16-ounce can jellied
cranberry sauce
2 3-ounce packages
raspberry gelatin

1 cup finely chopped nuts
1 cup (about) sugar

► Combine cranberry sauce and gelatin in saucepan.
► Bring to a boil, stirring constantly; remove from heat. Stir in nuts.
► Pour into greased 5x9-inch loaf pan. Chill, covered, overnight.
► Cut into 1x1½-inch pieces; roll in sugar.
► Chill for 24 hours; reroll in sugar.
► Store in refrigerator.
► Yields 2½ dozen.

HAYSTACKS

1 cup semisweet chocolate
chips
½ cup butterscotch chips

1 3-ounce can chow mein
noodles

► Combine chocolate and butterscotch chips in double boiler.
► Heat over hot water until melted, stirring occasionally; remove from heat. Stir in noodles.
► Drop by rounded teaspoonfuls onto waxed paper-lined cookie sheet. Let stand until firm.
► Yields 2 dozen.

POPCORN BALLS

8 cups popped popcorn
1⅓ cups chopped pecans
⅔ cup chopped almonds
1⅓ cups sugar

1 cup (2 sticks) margarine
½ cup light corn syrup
1 teaspoon vanilla extract

► Mix popcorn and nuts in large bowl.
► Combine sugar, margarine and corn syrup in medium saucepan. Cook for 5 minutes or until mixture turns light caramel color.
► Remove from heat; add vanilla. Pour over popcorn and nuts; mix well.
► Shape into balls with buttered hands; place on waxed paper to cool.
► Yields 10 servings.

DIPPING IN

These dips are very simple to make, but they don't have to look simple. The difference can be nothing more than creative serving. Try one of the following suggestions.

Scooped-Out Bread Loaf—Buy an unsliced round loaf of bread in the flavor you prefer. Hollow out loaf, leaving ¾-inch shell; cut top and scooped out bread pieces into cubes. Spoon dip into center of loaf. Serve with crackers and bread cubes for dipping or spreading. When the dip is gone, eat the bread bowl as well.

Pepper Shells—Cut off tops from firm peppers. Remove seed and membrane; spoon in dip.

Fruit Shells—Cut cantaloupe, honeydew or pineapple into halves; scoop out fruit in bite-sized chunks. Spoon dip into shells. Serve with fruit chunks.

ONION DIP

Combine 1 envelope dry onion soup mix and 2 cups sour cream in bowl. Mix well. Serve with chips or vegetables.

EASY DIP FOR VEGETABLES

Use your favorite salad dressing mix for this dip.

2 cups small-curd
  cottage cheese

8 ounces cream cheese
1 envelope salad dressing mix

► Combine cottage cheese, cream cheese and dry salad dressing mix in blender container; process until smooth.
► Spoon into serving bowl. Serve with bite-sized fresh vegetables such as broccoli, celery, carrots, cauliflower and cherry tomatoes.
► Yields 3 cups.

SWEET AND TART FRUIT DIP

1 cup plain yogurt
2 tablespoons honey

Juice and grated rind of 1 lemon

► Combine yogurt, honey, lemon juice and lemon rind in bowl; mix well.
► Chill overnight.
► Spoon into serving bowl; place in center of platter.
► Surround with wedges or bite-sized pieces of fresh fruit such as apple, pineapple, pear, peach or melon.
► Yields 1 cup.

CREAMY DIP FOR FRESH FRUIT

2 cups marshmallow creme
8 ounces cream cheese,
  softened

1 tablespoon grated
  orange rind
Ginger to taste

▶ Combine marshmallow creme and cream cheese in bowl; mix well.
▶ Add orange rind and ginger; mix well.
▶ Spoon into serving bowl; place on tray. Surround with fresh fruit such as strawberries, bananas or peach slices.
▶ Yields 3 cups.

SPINACH DIP

1   10-ounce package frozen
  chopped spinach, thawed
1 cup sour cream
1 cup mayonnaise
4 green onions, minced

1   8-ounce can water
  chestnuts, drained, chopped
1 package dry vegetable
  soup mix

▶ Squeeze moisture from thawed spinach. Drain on paper towel.
▶ Blend sour cream and mayonnaise in bowl.
▶ Add spinach, green onions, water chestnuts and dry vegetable soup mix; mix well.
▶ Chill for several hours to overnight. Spoon into serving bowl or hollowed-out bread loaf.
▶ Serve with crackers, bread cubes and fresh vegetables.
▶ Yields 3 cups.

TEX-MEX LAYERED DIP

2   10-ounce cans jalapeño
  bean dip
3 ripe avocados
2 tablespoons lemon juice
½ teaspoon salt
¼ teaspoon pepper
8 ounces sour cream
½ cup mayonnaise

1   (1½-ounce) package taco
  seasoning mix
1 cup minced onion
2 cups chopped tomatoes
1   3-ounce can chopped
  black olives, drained
2 cups shredded Cheddar or
  Monterey Jack cheese

▶ Spread bean dip evenly in large platter.
▶ Mash avocados with lemon juice, salt and pepper in bowl; spread carefully over bean layer.
▶ Mix sour cream, mayonnaise and taco seasoning mix in bowl; spread over avocado layer.
▶ Layer onion, tomatoes, olives and cheese over top.
▶ Serve with large tortilla chips.
▶ Yields 12 servings.

Tips From Dagwood

Sandwiches

MORE THAN YOU REALLY WANTED TO KNOW ABOUT SANDWICHES

Everyone knows a sandwich is just something to eat slapped between 2 pieces of bread.   Right ? — Wrong ! ! !

HOW TO MAKE A SANDWICH

*Before proceeding, answer the question "When will I eat this sandwich?" **Now, later** or **much later?** All three are handled differently.*

Now—Imagination knows no bounds. Add whatever meats, cheeses, salads, lettuce, tomatoes, seasonings and flights of fancy your mouth and tummy crave to 1 bread slice; top with the remaining slice. Cut into easy to eat pieces.

Later—A gap of several hours until lunchtime or this evening's study session means tomatoes, lettuce or similar ingredients that will wilt or become soggy on the bread or that will water down fillings, should be omitted or added just before serving. Put them in a baggie to take along.

Much Later—A period of days or even a couple of weeks between the building and the eating means restrictions including those mentioned above plus some care in selection of fillings. Obviously sandwiches intended for long-term storage must be frozen, so ingredients that cannot be frozen without changing in flavor or texture should be avoided. Most cheeses will taste the same but become crumbly; celery loses its crunch; and hard-boiled eggs become rubbery. Avoid using a lot of mayonnaise in all sandwich fillings.

Bonus Suggestion—A frozen sandwich added to a brown bag lunch will thaw by lunchtime in fresh tasty condition. Add a little package of lettuce, tomato, onion slices or pickles to your lunch and add pizazz to a sandwich built days ago.

FIRST THE BREAD

The outside of a sandwich is as variable as the inside. Try toasting the bread to any stage between lukewarm and charcoal that suits. Please be sure to toast before building the sandwich.

White bread
Whole wheat bread
Cracked wheat bread
Whole grain bread
Rye bread
Jewish rye bread
Swedish rye bread
Pumpernickel bread
Potato bread
Oat bread
Corn bread
Anadama bread
Soda bread
Sour dough bread
Italian bread
Raisin bread

Date nut bread
Cheese bread
Hawaiian bread
Thick-sliced bread
Thin-sliced bread
English muffins
Bagels—onion bagels, egg bagels, plain bagels
Hamburger buns
Biscuits
Tortillas—corn or flour
Pitas—white or whole wheat
French croissants
Kaiser rolls

▶ Use 2 adjoining slices from the loaf to make sure the slices are the same size and shape.
▶ Separate the 2 slices like opening a book, making sure the slices will fit back together.
▶ Spread softened butter, mayonnaise or cream cheese lightly over these surfaces to keep the bread from becoming soggy .

THEN THE FILLINGS

Sunshine—6 ounces of softened cream cheese or shredded cheese and ¼ cup raisins.

Tuna—6-ounce can drained water-pack tuna, 2 hard-boiled eggs, ¼ cup chopped celery, salt and pepper to taste and enough mayonnaise to bind.

Egg—6 hard-boiled eggs, minced onion, mustard, and salt and pepper to taste plus enough mayonnaise to bind.

Deviled Ham—4-ounce can deviled ham, 3 ounces softened cream cheese, 1 teaspoon horseradish and enough mayonnaise to bind.

Fruity Peanut Butter—1 cup creamy peanut butter, ½ cup chopped dates or raisins and ¼ cup chopped peanuts.

Crisp and Chunky—Chunky peanut butter and crispy crumbled bacon.

Chicken—7-ounce can chunk chicken, ¼ cup chopped celery, ¼ cup finely shredded carrot, salt and pepper to taste and enough mayonnaise to bind.

Hawaiian—1 cup pimento cheese and crushed pineapple

Ham Salad—1 cup ground ham, ¼ cup sweet pickle relish, salt, pepper and mustard to taste and enough mayonnaise to bind.

Dagwood—Meat loaf slices and catsup to taste (and mashed potatoes).

Roast Beef—Ground roast beef mixed with mustard or horseradish to taste and enough mayonnaise to bind.

BLT—Crisp-fried bacon, lettuce leaf and tomato slice.

Florida—Sliced avocado and Swiss cheese.

Boston—Mashed baked beans and coleslaw.

Meat Salads—See page 68.

BUNWICHES

Sloppy Joes—Mix some Ground Beef Scramble (page 92) with Sloppy Joe sauce. Spoon onto hamburger buns.

Deluxe Sloppy Joes—Top the Sloppy Joe mixture with a slice of cheese and 2 or more strips of crisp-fried bacon.

Barbecue—Spoon Barbecued Pork (page 22) onto hamburger buns.

ANYBODY'S FAVORITE BURGER

1 hamburger bun, split   1 hamburger patty (page 89)

► Toast or grill bun if desired.
► Place patty on bottom half of bun.
► Top patty with any favorite additions such as lettuce, tomato, onion, pickle, crisp-fried bacon, crumbled blue cheese, avocado slices, etc.
► For a cheeseburger, add a slice of Cheddar or Swiss cheese to the patty a minute or so before it is done to let cheese melt.

GRILLED CHEESE SANDWICH

Beware of "cheese" that does not melt. Not every product with a cheesy sounding name is the real thing. Some process cheeses, cheese foods, imitation cheeses and similar products may turn out to be inedible lumps that refuse to become gooey and delicious.

2 slices bread   1 tablespoon butter or
1 tablespoon mayonnaise   margarine, softened
1 slice cheese

► Spread 1 side of each bread slice with mayonnaise.
► Place cheese on 1 bread slice; top with remaining bread slice, mayonnaise side down. Spread top slice with half the butter.
► Preheat griddle or skillet over medium heat (on the stove) until a drop of water dropped on the hot griddle dances around and evaporates.
► Place sandwich buttered side down on the griddle.
► Cook until the buttered side is as brown as you like it (the cheese may have started to melt).
► Butter the bread slice on top; flip the sandwich.
► Cook until brown.
► Turn off burner and set griddle aside to cool.
► Remove sandwich to plate; cut in half.

VARIATIONS

Crunchy—Add pickles, potato chips or whatever you like. Cook as directed above. Eat immediately while warm and gooey.

Hearty—Add ham, bacon, tuna salad, chicken or use any kind of cheese including pimento or cream cheese. Cook as directed above. When the cupboard is almost bare even peanut butter is yummy grilled.

Pizza—Spread the bread with pizza sauce instead of mayonnaise and add several pepperoni slices on top of the cheese. Cook as directed above.

Checkered—For a sandwich that will astound your mother and amaze your friends, "grill" your sandwich in the family waffle iron (find the instruction book before attempting this, and use it).

OPEN-FACED SANDWICHES

An open-faced sandwich is considered in some circles to be easy on the diet (1 less bread slice could be a saving of as much as 100 calories) or even elegant (if it is pretty—cut into small pieces and arranged on a pretty plate). Anything that can go between 2 slices of bread can go on just one if the following cautions are observed.

▶ Do not stack stuff so high that it teeters precariously.
▶ Do not stack higher than your mouth will open.
▶ Do make it look pretty—remember without another bread slice, everything hangs out.

MANY DECKED SANDWICHES

A stack containing 3 or more slices of bread is another sandwich entirely (or almost 2). Follow the general instructions for a standard 2-slice sandwich adding fillings and bread alternately until sandwich reaches the altitude desired. Before attempting to cut the sandwich into pieces, secure by pinning long toothpicks through the layers in several places (the ones with the colored cellophane loops are pretty and probably won't be eaten by mistake).

CLUB SANDWICH

▶ Spread 3 slices plain or toasted bread with mayonnaise.
▶ Stack sandwich in the following order: bread, sliced chicken or turkey, bread, lettuce, tomato, 3 strips crisp-fried bacon and remaining bread.

REUBEN SANDWICH

▶ Spread 2 slices rye bread with Thousand Island salad dressing.
▶ Stack 1 slice bread, 1 slice Swiss cheese, 3 thin slices corned beef, about ¼ cup sauerkraut, another slice Swiss cheese and remaining bread.
▶ Grill in the same manner as for a grilled cheese sandwich.

PARTY POOR BOY

▶ Slice a long loaf of French bread horizontally from end to end. Spread the cut sides with mayonnaise or mustard.
▶ Stack layers of any combination of ham, turkey, pastrami, salami, corned beef, Cheddar cheese, Swiss cheese, Provolone cheese, sliced tomatoes, shredded lettuce, dill pickles, onion slices or green pepper rings on bottom half.
▶ Add the top. Cut across or diagonally into pieces.

Suggestion—Try doing a surprise sandwich for a party by having each guest bring something for the sandwich without knowing what others are bringing. Build it and what you see is what you get.

All Souped Up

Soups

As unbelievable and unlikely as it may seem, all soups do not come full grown from cans. However, many canned soups, when combined with other ingredients, provide a shortcut to comforting, tummy-warming lunches, suppers or even after-school pick-me-ups.

Soups can be steamy hot or icy cold, thick and stewy, or thin enough to sip from a glass; a hearty one-dish meal; a tasty extra with a sandwich; or an introduction to a many-course meal.

For your introduction to the wonderful world of soup-making, our recipes are quick, and most will require only 30 minutes from can opener to bowl. They are also easy to prepare, most using only one saucepan for easy clean-up. And, of course, they are yummy, or why bother to make them?

SOUPER TOPPERS

Sprinkle one of these toppings below on your soup for an attractive and tasty garnish.

Popped popcorn
Grated cheese
Seasoned croutons
French-fried onions
Matchstick potatoes
Sour cream or yogurt
Goldfish crackers

Oyster crackers
Rice chex
Party mix
Cheese puffs
Potato chips
Cheese toast
Pretzels

QUICKIE SOUPS

The following quickie soups require only 2 cans of condensed soup and a pan plus a stove and water or a bit of milk. Just open the cans, empty into the saucepan, stir in the water or milk gradually and bring to a simmer over medium heat, stirring occasionally.

Asparagus—Cheddar cheese soup, cream of asparagus soup, 1 soup can water and 1 soup can milk.

Bean—Bean with bacon soup, tomato-rice soup and 2 soup cans water.

Beefy—Chili beef soup, vegetable beef soup and 2 soup cans water.

Cheesy—Cheddar cheese soup, tomato soup, 1 soup can water and 1 soup can milk.

Chicken—Chicken vegetable soup, cream of chicken soup, 1 soup can water and 1 soup can milk.

Clam—Clam chowder, cream of mushroom soup, 1 soup can water and 1 soup can milk.

San Juan—Black bean soup, mushroom soup and 2 soup cans water.

COLD ASPARAGUS SOUP

Cold soups add an elegant touch.

1 10-ounce can condensed cream of asparagus soup
1 cup sour cream
1 cup milk
1 cup crushed ice
3 drops (or more) Tabasco sauce

▶ Combine undiluted soup, and remaining ingredients in blender container.
▶ Process for 20 seconds or until smooth.
▶ Pour into small soup bowls or serve in cups or mugs.
▶ Yields 4 to 6 servings.

MAKE-AHEAD GAZPACHO

1 10-ounce can condensed Spanish-style vegetable soup
¾ cup V-8 or tomato juice
1 tablespoon olive oil
1 clove of garlic, minced
1 tablespoon lemon juice
⅛ teaspoon black pepper
⅓ cup chopped green pepper or cucumber

▶ Mix undiluted soup with remaining ingredients in bowl.
▶ Cover bowl tightly. Chill for 4 hours. Ladle into soup bowls.
▶ Garnish each serving with croutons and serve immediately.
▶ Yields 3 servings.

HEARTY BROCCOLI SOUP

1 10-ounce package frozen chopped broccoli
1 tablespoon dried onion
2 cups milk

2 10-ounce cans condensed cream of potato soup
½ cup shredded Swiss cheese

► Cook broccoli according to the directions on the package using a 3-quart saucepan and adding the dried onion to the water.
► Remove from heat but do not drain.
► Stir in milk and undiluted soup; mix well.
► Heat to serving temperature over medium heat, stirring frequently.
► Ladle into soup bowls; sprinkle cheese on top.
► Yields 6 servings.

EASY CHEESY CHICKEN-VEGETABLE SOUP

3 10-ounce cans condensed chicken broth
2 soup cans water
1 tablespoon dried onion flakes

2 7-ounce cans chicken
2 10-ounce packages frozen mixed vegetables
1 8-ounce jar Cheez Whiz
½ cup milk

► Combine broth and water in 3-quart saucepan. Bring to a boil over medium-high heat. Add onion flakes, chicken and frozen vegetables. Return to a boil, stirring occasionally. Cover and reduce heat to medium-low.
► Simmer for about 10 minutes or until vegetables are tender. Add Cheez Whiz and milk. Cook until Cheez Whiz melts, stirring constantly.
► Ladle into soup bowls. Serve with crackers or hot buttered bread.
► Yields 6 to 8 servings.

MOCK MINESTRONE

½ pound ground beef
¾ cup chopped onion
1 10-ounce can condensed tomato soup
1 10-ounce can condensed vegetable soup

1 16-ounce can pinto beans
1 10-ounce can condensed beef bouillon
1 soup can water
1 cup thin spaghetti, broken into 1 to 2-inch pieces

► Cook ground beef with onion according to directions on page 92.
► Combine condensed tomato soup, vegetable soup and beans in 3-quart saucepan. Add bouillon and water gradually, mixing well.
► Bring to a boil over medium-high heat, stirring frequently. Add ground beef; return to a boil. Add spaghetti; mix well.
► Cook for 10 minutes, stirring frequently. Ladle into soup bowls.
► Yields 6 servings.

POTATO AND HOT DOG CHOWDER

3 cups water
1 5½-ounce package dry
   scalloped potato mix
1 10-ounce package frozen
   mixed vegetables

3 cups milk
4 hot dogs, sliced into rounds
¼ cup Parmesan cheese

▶ Bring water to a boil in 3-quart saucepan over medium-high heat. Add dry potato mix and frozen vegetables. Return to a boil; cover and reduce heat to medium-low.
▶ Simmer for 15 minutes, stirring about every 5 minutes. Add milk and hot dogs; mix well. Bring to the simmering point over medium heat, stirring every minute or two.
▶ Simmer for 10 minutes longer, stirring occasionally.
▶ Ladle into soup bowls; sprinkle with cheese.
▶ Yields 6 servings.

TEN-MINUTE VEGETABLE-BEEF SOUP

1 pound ground beef
1 16-ounce can mixed
   vegetables, drained

1 10-ounce can condensed
   cream of mushroom soup
3 6-ounce cans V-8 juice

▶ Cook and drain ground beef according to directions on page 92.
▶ Combine ground beef with vegetables, mushroom soup and enough V-8 juice to make soup of desired thickness in 3-quart saucepan; mix well.
▶ Bring to a simmer over medium-high heat, stirring every minute or two.
▶ Ladle into soup bowls. Serve with crackers.
▶ Yields 6 servings.

CREAMY CORN CHOWDER

4 cups frozen hashed
   brown potatoes
½ cup chopped onion
¼ cup margarine
1 cup water
3 cups milk

1 12-ounce can whole
   kernel corn
Salt and pepper to taste
½ cup shredded Cheddar
   cheese

▶ Combine frozen potatoes, onion, margarine and water in 3-quart saucepan. Bring to a boil over medium-high heat. Cover and reduce heat to medium-low.
▶ Simmer for 10 minutes or until potatoes are tender. Add milk and corn. Bring to the simmering point; season with salt and pepper. Simmer for 10 minutes longer, stirring occasionally.
▶ Ladle into soup bowls; sprinkle with cheese.
▶ Yields 6 to 8 servings.

RAVIOLI SOUP

1 10-ounce can condensed beef broth	1 10-ounce package frozen peas and carrots
1 cup tomato juice	½ cup chopped onion
3 cups water	1 teaspoon salt
1 cup frozen hashed brown potatoes	¼ teaspoon pepper
	1 15-ounce can ravioli

► Combine broth, tomato juice and water in 3-cup saucepan. Bring to a boil over medium-high heat. Add potatoes, peas and carrots, onion, salt and pepper. Return to a boil. Cover and reduce heat to medium-low.
► Simmer for 7 minutes or until vegetables are tender. Add ravioli with sauce. Simmer for 10 minutes longer, stirring occasionally.
► Ladle into soup bowls. Garnish with Parmesan cheese.
► Yields 6 to 8 servings.

MEXICAN MIX-UP

1 10-ounce can condensed bean with bacon soup	1 12-ounce can Mexicorn
1 soup can water	⅛ teaspoon garlic powder
	⅛ teaspoon Tabasco sauce

► Combine bean soup and water in 2-quart saucepan over medium heat. Bring to the simmering point, stirring frequently.
► Add Mexicorn, garlic powder and Tabasco sauce; mix well. Heat to serving temperature, stirring frequently.
► Ladle into soup bowls. Serve with taco chips.
► Yields 2 servings.

CHUNKY CHEESE SOUP

4 cups frozen hashed brown potatoes	6 cups canned chicken broth
1 cup chopped onion	2 10-ounce cans condensed cream of chicken or cream of potato soup
1 16-ounce package frozen mixed vegetables	1½ pounds Velveeta cheese

► Combine potatoes, onion, mixed vegetables and broth in 6-quart saucepan. Bring to a boil over medium-high heat; cover and reduce heat. Simmer for 15 minutes.
► Add soup; mix well. Bring to a simmer, stirring frequently. Cut cheese into 1-inch cubes; add several at a time to hot soup. Cook until cheese melts, stirring constantly. Ladle into soup bowls.
► Yields 8 servings.

Suggestion—If you have a Crock•Pot, just mix up everything except the cheese in it. Plug it in, set on Low and don't forget the cover. In about 6 hours add the cheese as above. This method takes longer but is easier.

The Supertastiks

Salads

Just think—a salad bar with all your favorite things right in your own home! Combinations you have dreamed about. The fixings are endless and can be fun to plan. In these recipes are some new suggestions for making your salad bar even better. Starting with the basics, look at the list of salad greens available, then the "fixins" and toppings to add taste treats to your salad for all seasons. Include in your "dream bar" our pasta salads and sweet salads to complete your meal. Delicious!

GREEN SALADS

*Wash salad greens just as you are ready to use them. Drain well so the dressing will cling and not drip off. Try a salad spinner for this; it's quick and thorough. Always **tear** salad greens apart. Cutting with a knife causes discoloration. To revive wilted salad greens, dip in hot water, then into ice water mixed with a little lemon juice; drain. Instant perked-up greens!*

SALAD GREENS

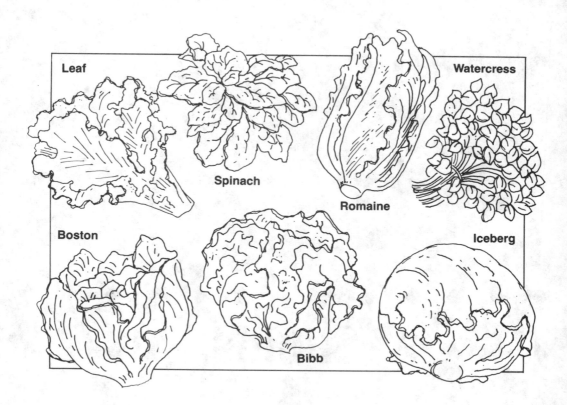

Leaf

Spinach

Romaine

Watercress

Boston

Bibb

Iceberg

SALAD "FIXINS"

Alfalfa sprouts
Artichoke hearts
Asparagus
Bamboo shoots
Bean sprouts
Broccoli
Cabbage, green and red
Carrots
Cauliflower
Celery
Cheese
Chicken
Chives
Crab meat
Cucumbers
Garbanzo beans

Green peppers
Ham
Hard-boiled eggs
Hearts of palm
Mushrooms
Olives, black and green
Onions
Radishes
Red peppers
Salami
Shrimp
Tomatoes
Water chestnuts
Yellow peppers
Yellow squash
Zucchini

SALAD TOPPINGS

Bacon bits
Chow mein noodles
Croutons

French-fried onions
Potato sticks
Sunflower seed

SALAD DRESSINGS

A most important part of your salad is the salad dressing. It should complement the other ingredients and enhance the flavors of all. Use your favorite prepared dressing or try one of these.

Thousand Island—Combine mayonnaise, chili sauce, pickle relish and chopped hard-boiled egg.

Lemon-Herb—Mix your favorite herb or herb vinegar with lemon juice.

Cranberry—Blend 1 cup cranberry sauce, 1 cup mayonnaise and 2 tablespoons lime juice.

French—Combine ½ cup oil, ½ cup vinegar, 3 tablespoons sugar, 3 tablespoons catsup and ½ teaspoon dry mustard.

Blue Cheese—Process 1 cup cottage cheese, 4 cups milk and 4 teaspoons lemon juice in blender until smooth. Add ⅓ cup blue cheese.

Spicy Nectar—Combine 1 cup sour cream, ½ cup apricot nectar, ½ cup oil, 2 tablespoons sugar and ½ teaspoon paprika.

Honey-Mustard—Combine ⅓ cup honey, 1 or more teaspoons dry mustard, ⅓ cup vinegar, ¼ cup sugar and 1 cup oil.

FOUR-BEAN SALAD

1 16-ounce can cut
  green beans
1 16-ounce can cut
  wax beans
1 16-ounce can fordhook
  lima beans

1 16-ounce can red
  kidney beans
1 onion, sliced into rings
½ cup chopped green pepper
1 recipe Basic Sweet-Sour
  Marinade and Dressing

▶ Drain beans; rinse and drain kidney beans. Combine beans, onion and green pepper in bowl.
▶ Add Dressing; mix well. Marinate in refrigerator for 12 hours to 1 week.
▶ Yields 8½ cups.

BASIC SWEET-SOUR MARINADE AND DRESSING

1 cup vinegar
¾ cup sugar

¾ cup oil
Salt and pepper to taste

▶ Combine all 5 ingredients in bowl; mix well.
▶ Use with Four-Bean Salad, broccoli, cauliflower, mushrooms or other vegetables.
▶ Yields 2½ cups.

MARINATED CARROT SALAD

2 pounds carrots
1 medium onion, sliced
  into rings

1 green pepper, chopped
1 recipe Basic Tomato
  Marinade and Dressing

▶ Scrape carrots and slice thinly. Combine with water to cover in saucepan. Cook for 10 minutes or just until tender; drain.
▶ Combine carrots, onion and green pepper in bowl. Add Basic Tomato Marinade and Dressing; mix well. Chill, covered, for 24 hours to 2 weeks.
▶ Yields 8 servings.

BASIC TOMATO MARINADE AND DRESSING

1 10-ounce can condensed
  tomato soup
½ cup oil
¾ cup sugar
¾ cup vinegar

1 teaspoon Worcestershire
  sauce
1 teaspoon prepared mustard
Salt and pepper to taste

▶ Combine soup, oil, sugar and vinegar in bowl or jar; mix well.
▶ Stir in Worcestershire sauce, mustard, salt and pepper.
▶ Store in airtight container in refrigerator.
▶ Use as marinade/dressing for carrots or other vegetables.
▶ Yields 3 cups.

CARROT SALAD

3 cups shredded carrots
½ cup raisins

½ cup crushed pineapple
½ cup mayonnaise

▶ Combine carrots, raisins and pineapple in bowl.
▶ Add mayonnaise; mix well. Chill for several hours.
▶ Yields 4 to 6 servings.

BASIC COLESLAW

4 cups shredded cabbage or
  1 package shredded
  cabbage

1 recipe Basic
  Coleslaw Dressing

▶ Combine cabbage and Dressing in bowl; mix well. Chill in refrigerator.
▶ Yields 6 to 8 servings.

VARIATIONS

Two-Tone—Substitute 1 cup shredded red cabbage for 1 cup shredded green cabbage. Mix as directed above.

Confetti—Add ¼ cup shredded carrot and ¼ cup chopped green or red pepper. Mix as directed above.

South Seas—Add ¾ cup crushed pineapple, ½ cup mandarin oranges and ¼ cup chopped water chestnuts. Mix as directed above.

Harvest—Add ½ cup grated apple and ¼ cup raisins. Mix as directed above.

Tropical—Add 1 finely chopped banana and ½ cup seeded grape halves. Mix as directed above.

Spicy—Add ½ cup sliced radishes. Mix as directed above.

Easy—Substitute bottled coleslaw dressing or poppy seed dressing.

BASIC COLESLAW DRESSING

3 heaping tablespoons
  mayonnaise
3 tablespoons sugar
3 tablespoons white vinegar
3 tablespoons water

½ teaspoon prepared mustard
  (optional)
Salt and pepper to taste
  (optional)

▶ Combine all ingredients in jar; cover. Shake to mix well.
▶ Store in airtight container in refrigerator.
▶ Yields ¾ cup.

CORN SALAD

2   16-ounce cans Mexicorn
1 green pepper, chopped
1 onion, chopped
1 cucumber, chopped

1 tomato, chopped
1   12-ounce bottle of
     Catalina salad dressing
Garlic salt to taste

▶ Drain Mexicorn well. Combine with pepper, onion, cucumber and tomato in serving bowl.
▶ Add salad dressing and garlic salt; mix well. Chill overnight.
▶ Yields 8 servings.

CUCUMBER AND ONION SALAD

4 large cucumbers, peeled,
   sliced
2 medium onions, sliced
   into rings

½ teaspoon sugar
Salt and white pepper to taste
1 cup sour cream

▶ Soak cucumber in salted water to cover for several hours; drain.
▶ Combine cucumbers, onions, sugar, salt and white pepper in bowl.
▶ Add sour cream; mix gently. Let stand for several hours.
▶ Yields 8 servings.

VARIATION
Marinate cucumbers and onions in Basic Sweet-Sour Marinade and Dressing (page 62) for 8 hours or longer for a different taste.

GREEN PEA SALAD

1   10-ounce package
   frozen green peas
½ cup chopped cashews
½ cup chopped celery

2 tablespoons grated onion
¼ teaspoon salt
½ cup sour cream

▶ Thaw peas under hot running water; drain well. Combine with cashews, celery, onion and salt in bowl. Add sour cream; mix gently.
▶ Chill for several hours. Spoon into lettuce cups on salad plates.
▶ Yields 4 to 6 servings.

VARIATION
Substitute peanuts, water chestnuts or small cubes of Cheddar cheese for cashews and/or ½ cup mayonnaise and 1 teaspoon prepared mustard for sour cream.

POTATO SALAD

6 medium potatoes
3 hard-boiled eggs, chopped
½ cup chopped celery
½ cup chopped green pepper
½ cup chopped dill pickle
½ cup salad olives

1 teaspoon salt
½ teaspoon pepper
¼ teaspoon garlic powder
¼ teaspoon celery salt
1 cup mayonnaise
1 tablespoon prepared mustard

► Place potatoes in water to cover in saucepan. Cook over medium heat until potatoes are tender; drain and cool. Peel and chop potatoes.
► Mix potatoes, eggs, celery, green pepper, pickle and olives in bowl.
► Add salt, pepper, garlic powder, celery salt, mayonnaise and mustard; mix well. Chill for several hours.
► Yields 6½ cups.

BASIC AMBROSIA

Orange sections
Coconut
Pineapple chunks (optional)
Kiwifruit (optional)

Grapefruit sections (optional)
Grape halves (optional)
Cherries (optional)

► Combine all ingredients in bowl.
► Chill until serving time.

CHERRY FLUFF

1   21-ounce can cherry
    pie filling
1   20-ounce can crushed
    pineapple, drained
1   14-ounce can sweetened
    condensed milk

1   10-ounce package
    miniature marshmallows
1   12-ounce carton
    whipped topping

► Combine pie filling, crushed pineapple and sweetened condensed milk in bowl; mix well. Fold in marshmallows and whipped topping.
► Chill in refrigerator overnight or freeze in paper-lined muffin cups.
► Yields 16 servings.

WALDORF SALAD

3 cups chopped apples
½ cup raisins

½ cup broken walnuts
½ cup mayonnaise

► Combine apples, raisins and walnuts in bowl. Add mayonnaise; mix well.
► Chill in refrigerator until serving time. Spoon into lettuce cups.
► Yields 6 servings.

GELATIN SALADS

*There are two kinds of gelatin: Flavored gelatin like Jell-O and un-flavored gelatin, like Knox. Both will congeal mixtures but are used a little differently. Unflavored gelatin must be softened in a small amount of **cold** water, then heated until dissolved. Flavored gelatin is added to **boiling** water and stirred until completely dissolved. Any undissolved gelatin sinks to the bottom of the bowl and becomes rubbery as it congeals.*

TIPS TO REMEMBER ABOUT GELATIN

Fruits—Add fruits and nuts to gelatin when partially congealed so the added ingredients will stay evenly distributed in the mold rather than sinking to the bottom. Do not use fresh pineapple or kiwifruit.

Congealing—Never freeze gelatin in order to hurry its setting because when the gelatin thaws, it turns to water and will never congeal again.

Unmolding—To unmold gelatin, let it stand at room temperature for several minutes. Dip the mold briefly, *almost* to the rim, in warm water. Place your serving plate on top of the mold, and invert the whole thing. Shake with an up and down motion to loosen, then remove mold. Add greens as garnish.

CONGEALED ORANGE SALAD

1   6-ounce package orange
    gelatin
2 cups boiling water
1 pint orange sherbet

1 cup orange juice
1   16-ounce can mandarin
    oranges, drained

▶ Dissolve gelatin in boiling water in bowl, stirring constantly. Stir in orange sherbet and orange juice.
▶ Chill until partially set. Stir in oranges; pour into mold.
▶ Chill until set. Unmold onto serving plate.
▶ Yield: 8 to 12 servings.

CONGEALED CRANBERRY SALAD

1   6-ounce package
    raspberry gelatin
1½ cups boiling water
1   16-ounce can whole
    cranberry sauce

1 cup chopped celery
1   8-ounce can crushed
    pineapple, partially drained
1 cup chopped pecans

▶ Dissolve gelatin in 1½ cups boiling water in bowl. Add cranberry sauce. Chill until partially set. Add celery, pineapple and pecans; mix well.
▶ Spoon into mold. Chill until firm. Unmold onto serving plate.
▶ Yields 8 servings.

PASTA SALADS

Chilled pasta salads have become really popular as main dish salads or as complements to other dishes. These offer a wonderful opportunity to try different combinations of pastas, vegetables, meats and dressings.

THE PASTA

Bow ties	Three-color rotini
Elbow macaroni	Wheels
Shells	Ziti

THE SUPPLEMENTS

Cheddar cheese	Bologna	Crab meat
Mozzarella cheese	Chicken	Lobster
Parmesan cheese	Ham	Salmon
Provolone cheese	Salami	Shrimp
Swiss cheese	Turkey	Tuna

THE VEGETABLES

Black olives	Green peas	Mushrooms
Broccoli	Green peppers	Onions
Celery	Hearts of palm	Parsley
Cherry tomatoes	Italian-style beans	Radishes
Cucumbers	Kidney beans	Red peppers
Garbanzo beans	Marinated artichokes	Yellow squash
Green olives	Marinated mushrooms	Zucchini

THE SEASONINGS

Basil	Marjoram	Pepper
Celery seed	Onion Powder	Rosemary
Garlic powder	Oregano	Salt
Italian seasoning	Paprika	Thyme

THE DRESSINGS

Italian salad dressing	Marinade from mushrooms
Lemon juice	Mayonnaise
Marinade from artichokes	Olive oil and vinegar

CHICKEN SALAD

2 cups chopped cooked
  chicken (page 100)
½ cup chopped celery
¾ cup green grape halves

½ cup chopped pecans
6 tablespoons mayonnaise
Salt and pepper to taste
Paprika

▶ Combine chicken, celery, grapes and pecans in bowl.
▶ Add mayonnaise, salt and pepper; mix well. Sprinkle with paprika. Chill until serving time.
▶ Yields 4 to 6 servings.

HAM SALAD

2   7-ounce cans chunk ham,
  drained
½ cup drained crushed
  pineapple

½ cup chopped celery
¼ cup raisins
6 tablespoons mayonnaise
1 teaspoon dry mustard

▶ Combine ham, pineapple, celery and raisins in bowl.
▶ Add mayonnaise and dry mustard; mix well. Chill until serving time.
▶ Yields 4 servings.

TUNA SALAD

1   6-ounce can tuna
  packed in water
¼ cup chopped apple
¼ cup chopped celery

¼ cup mayonnaise
1 tablespoon lemon juice
Salt and pepper to taste

▶ Drain tuna. Combine tuna, apple and celery in bowl.
▶ Add mayonnaise, lemon juice, salt and pepper; mix well. Chill for 1 hour.
▶ Yields 2 servings.

SHRIMP AND RICE SALAD

1 package long grain and
  wild rice mix
1 pound peeled cooked
  shrimp

1 cup chopped celery
½ cup chopped almonds
1 cup mayonnaise
1 tablespoon lemon juice

▶ Cook rice mix according to package directions.
▶ Combine rice with shrimp, celery, almonds, mayonnaise and lemon juice in bowl. Chill in refrigerator.
▶ Yields 4 servings.

Catsup Is Not A Vegetable!

Vegetables

Vegetables have come of age! There was a time when only Popeye and the hungry children in China loved spinach, but with today's emphasis on slim figures and health, we know that veggies are a great way to fill up without filling out. It's no coincidence that most of our favorite fast food restaurants have vegetable and salad bars.

Even cooked vegetables are tasty and easy to do. The ultra easy way, of course, starts with frozen vegetables. There are great vegetable mixtures, some including pasta or rice, which need only the addition of shrimp or chicken for a complete—and completely easy—meal. The only tricky part is following the package directions.

Fresh vegetables can be easy also, once you solve the mysteries of the produce department. Our recipes emphasize choosing, preparing, cooking and serving fresh vegetables. Our simple, all-purpose sauces and garnishes can transform your plain vegetables into gourmet treats.

BUTTER SAUCES

Mix ¼ cup melted butter with 1 of the following seasonings.

1 tablespoon horseradish	¼ cup chopped walnuts or
½ teaspoon dry mustard	almonds
1 to 2 tablespoons orange	1 tablespoon chopped parsley
juice concentrate	¾ teaspoon dillweed plus
¼ teaspoon garlic powder	⅛ teaspoon garlic powder
¼ teaspoon onion powder	2 tablespoons sesame seed plus
1 tablespoon fresh lemon juice	2 tablespoons lemon juice

CREAM SAUCES

Cream Cheese Sauce—Melt 3 ounces cream cheese with ½ cup evaporated milk in saucepan over low heat.

White Sauce—Blend 1½ tablespoons flour with 1½ tablespoons melted butter and 1 cup milk in saucepan. Cook until thickened, stirring constantly.

CHEESE SAUCES

Rich Cheese Sauce—Add Parmesan cheese or shredded Cheddar, Swiss or Monterey Jack cheese to Cream Cheese Sauce or White Sauce.

Easy Cheese Sauce—Heat cheese soup or Cheez Whiz until bubbly.

HOLLANDAISE SAUCES

Classic Hollandaise Sauce—Combine 3 beaten egg yolks and 2 tablespoons lemon juice in saucepan. Place over hot water in double boiler. Add 1 stick butter ⅓ at a time, beating constantly until thickened.

Mock Hollandaise Sauce—Blend 4 ounces softened cream cheese, 1 tablespoon lemon juice and 1 egg yolk. Serve cold over hot vegetables.

ASPARAGUS

Choose firm straight stalks with compact tips. Store in refrigerator for up to 2 days. Break off stalks as close to bottom as possible where they snap easily. Leave stalks whole or cut into 1-inch pieces. One pound of asparagus makes 4 servings.

Stove Top—Place fresh asparagus on rack in saucepan with 1 inch boiling water or tie stalks into bundle and stand in 1 inch boiling water. Steam, tightly covered, for 8 minutes for cut pieces or 10 minutes for stalks.

Microwave—Place in shallow glass dish with ¼ cup water. Microwave, tightly covered, on High for 6 to 9 minutes or until tender-crisp. Let stand, covered, for 3 minutes before draining and serving.

Serving Suggestions
► Serve asparagus cold or hot with sesame or walnut butter (page 70) or Hollandaise sauce.
► Roll 1 or 2 cooked asparagus stalks in thin slices of boiled ham and place in single layer in baking pan. Top with Rich Cheese Sauce. Broil until heated through.
► Layer cooked asparagus, ham and sliced cheese or cheese sauce on toast or English muffin. Broil until bubbly.

ASPARAGUS CASSEROLE

2   16-ounce cans
asparagus spears
1   7-ounce can sliced water
chestnuts
1   8-ounce can sliced
mushrooms

1   2-ounce jar chopped
pimento
1   10-ounce can condensed
cream of mushroom soup
4 hard-boiled eggs, sliced

▶ Preheat oven to 350 degrees. Drain asparagus, water chestnuts, mushrooms and pimento.
▶ Mix water chestnuts, mushrooms, pimento and soup in bowl.
▶ Layer asparagus and eggs in greased 1½-quart casserole. Spoon soup mixture over top. Bake for 30 minutes.
▶ Yields 8 servings.

DRIED BEANS

Dried beans—and peas—are found in packages on the market shelf. The dozens of kinds include black beans, black-eyed peas, Great Northern beans, kidney beans, lentils, lima beans, pinto beans and split peas. Each 1 cup dried beans yields 2 to 2½ cups cooked beans.

Stove Top—Sort dried beans and discard shriveled beans. Rinse well. Combine each cup of dried beans with 2 to 3 cups water in saucepan. Bring to a full rolling boil over high heat, cover the pan and remove from heat. Let stand for 1 to 2 hours. Drain soaking water and add fresh water to cover generously. Simmer for 1 to 2 hours or until beans are tender. Add 1 teaspoon salt for each cup of uncooked beans. Add ham, onion, garlic or bay leaf if desired. Cook for several minutes longer.

BOSTON BAKED BEANS

2   16-ounce packages
dried navy beans
¾ cup dark molasses
½ cup packed brown sugar

1 onion, chopped
1 tablespoon dry mustard
1 teaspoon pepper
8 ounces salt pork, cut up

▶ Soak beans according to instructions above. Do not drain. Preheat oven to 250 degrees.
▶ Combine beans with molasses, brown sugar, onion, dry mustard, pepper and salt pork in Dutch oven; mix well. Bring to a boil.
▶ Bake beans, covered, for 7 hours, adding additional water if beans become dry.
▶ Yields 12 servings.

EASY BAKED BEANS

1 29-ounce can pork and
    beans
½ cup chopped onion
¼ cup chopped green pepper
3 tablespoons brown sugar
1 tablespoon prepared
    mustard

3 tablespoons catsup
1 tablespoon Worcestershire
    sauce
Salt and cayenne pepper to
    taste
4 slices bacon

▶ Preheat oven to 350 degrees.
▶ Combine beans, onion and green pepper in bowl. Add brown sugar, mustard, catsup, Worcestershire sauce, salt and cayenne pepper; mix well.
▶ Spoon into 2-quart baking dish. Top with bacon. Bake for 1½ hours.
▶ Yields 8 servings.

GREEN BEANS

Store green beans in the refrigerator for up to 2 days. Wash beans when ready to cook. Snap off ends, pulling off any strings. Leave beans whole, cut into pieces or slice thinly end to end (French style). One pound of beans makes 4 servings.

Stove Top—Bring 1 inch salted water to a boil in saucepan. Add beans, chopped onion, dill, hot pepper or ham if desired; cover pan and reduce heat. Cook whole or cut beans for 30 minutes or until tender. Cook French-style green beans for 12 minutes or until tender.

Microwave—Place beans in glass dish with ¼ cup water. Microwave, covered, on High for 10 to 15 minutes, stirring once. Let beans stand, covered, for 3 minutes.

Serving Suggestions
▶ Serve with almond or mustard butter (page 70) or cream cheese sauce (page 71) mixed with 2 teaspoons horseradish.
▶ Toss warm drained beans with Italian salad dressing and sesame seed.

SWEET AND SOUR GREEN BEANS

2 10-ounce packages
    French-style green beans
6 slices bacon
½ cup chopped onion

¼ cup slivered almonds
¼ cup vinegar
1 tablespoon sugar

▶ Cook green beans according to package directions; drain.
▶ Fry bacon in skillet until crisp. Remove to paper towel to drain; crumble.
▶ Sauté onion and almonds in bacon drippings in skillet until transparent. Add vinegar and sugar; mix well.
▶ Add beans. Cook until heated through. Sprinkle with bacon.
▶ Yields 6 servings.

GREEN BEAN CASSEROLE

2 16-ounce cans cut or
   French-style green beans,
   drained
½ cup milk
1 10-ounce can condensed
   cream of mushroom soup

¼ cup slivered almonds
Pepper to taste
1 cup shredded Cheddar
   cheese (optional)
½ 3-ounce can French-fried
   onions

▶ Preheat oven to 350 degrees.
▶ Mix beans, milk, soup, almonds, pepper and cheese in bowl.
▶ Spoon into greased 1½-quart baking dish. Bake for 30 minutes.
▶ Sprinkle French-fried onions over top. Bake for 5 minutes longer.
▶ Yields 6 servings.

BROCCOLI

Choose stalks with dark green, tightly closed flowerets. Store in plastic bag in the refrigerator. Serve cooked or uncooked. Wash broccoli, removing outer leaves and tough ends of stalks. Split stalks lengthwise into uniform spears, or cut into flowerets. One pound makes 4 servings.

Stove Top—Cook broccoli in 1 inch boiling water in covered saucepan over low heat for 8 to 10 minutes or until tender-crisp; drain.

Microwave—Microwave broccoli in ¼ cup water in covered shallow glass dish on High for 8 minutes or until tender-crisp. Let stand for 3 minutes.

Serving Suggestions
▶ Serve hot with lemon butter (page 70) or cheese sauce (page 71).
▶ Microwave with ½ cup chopped red onion and ¾ cup Italian salad dressing instead of water. Sprinkle with Parmesan cheese.
▶ Serve hot with mixture of ½ cup sour cream, 1 teaspoon horseradish and ½ teaspoon prepared mustard.

BROCCOLI AND RICE CASSEROLE

2 10-ounce packages
   frozen chopped broccoli
1 cup uncooked minute rice
1 8-ounce jar Cheez Whiz

1 10-ounce can condensed
   cream of celery soup
1 cup cornflake crumbs

▶ Preheat oven to 325 degrees. Thaw broccoli.
▶ Combine broccoli, rice, Cheez Whiz and soup in bowl; mix well.
▶ Spoon into 1½-quart casserole. Top with crumbs. Bake for 1 hour or until rice is tender.
▶ Yields 8 servings.

CARROTS

Choose crisp bright orange carrots. Remove tops and store in refrigerator for up to 2 weeks. Serve cooked or uncooked. Wash carrots and scrape or peel thinly with vegetable peeler. Cook small carrots whole. Slice, chop, cut into strips or shred larger carrots. One pound makes 4 servings.

Stove Top—Cook carrots, covered, in ½-inch boiling water in saucepan for 15 to 20 minutes for whole carrots or 10 to 15 minutes for cut carrots.

Microwave—Place cut carrots in 2 tablespoons water in shallow glass dish. Microwave, covered, on High for 5 to 7 minutes or until tender-crisp.

Serving Suggestions
► Serve carrots with a glaze of ¼ cup melted butter, 1 tablespoon sugar and ½ teaspoon nutmeg or ginger.
► Serve with orange butter (page 70) and orange sections.
► Serve chilled with Italian salad dressing and dillweed to taste.

GLAZED CARROTS

2 cups sliced carrots
3 tablespoons butter
2 tablespoons sugar

Juice of ½ lemon
½ teaspoon paprika

► Cook carrots according to directions above; drain.
► Combine butter, sugar, lemon juice and paprika in skillet. Heat over medium heat until bubbly. Add carrots.
► Cook for 8 to 10 minutes or until glazed, stirring constantly.
► Yields 3 to 4 servings.

CAULIFLOWER

Choose heavy compact heads with uniform flowerets. Sprinkle leaves with water and store whole head in refrigerator for up to 5 days. Cook cauliflower whole or cut into flowerets. One head of cauliflower will make 6 servings.

Stove Top—Simmer in 1 inch water in covered saucepan for 15 minutes for whole cauliflower, 8 minutes for flowerets, or until tender-crisp.

Microwave—Microwave cauliflower with 2 tablespoons water in covered glass dish on High for 5 minutes or until tender. Let stand for 3 minutes.

Serving Suggestions
► Mix with Cream Sauce (page 71), sprinkle with bread crumbs and bake at 350 degrees until bubbly.
► Marinate raw or cooked cauliflower in Basic Sweet-Sour Marinade and Dressing (page 62) for 24 hours.

CONFETTI CAULIFLOWER

This is a pretty holiday dish.

1 large head cauliflower
1   4-ounce jar whipped
    cream cheese with pimento
1 tablespoon milk
¼ teaspoon (or more) dry
    mustard
¼ teaspoon salt
Chopped chives

▶ Separate cauliflower into flowerets. Cook as directed on page 75.
▶ Combine cream cheese, milk, dry mustard and salt in saucepan. Heat to serving temperature, stirring to blend well.
▶ Drain cauliflower well. Place in serving dish. Spoon sauce over top. Sprinkle with chives.
▶ Yields 6 servings.

CORN

Choose ears of corn with even rows of plump kernels and fresh green husks. Use corn as soon as possible. Store in husks in refrigerator. Remove husks and silk from ears just before cooking. Brush with soft vegetable brush to remove hard to reach silk. Cook ears whole or cut kernels from cobs.

Stove Top—Cook ears of corn in boiling water in large covered saucepan over medium heat for 6 to 10 minutes or until tender.

Microwave—Microwave ears of corn with ¼ cup water in covered shallow glass dish on High for 7 minutes for 2 ears or 12 minutes for 4 ears.

Serving Suggestions
▶ Serve corn with butter flavored with chili powder, parsley, dill or chives.
▶ To butter, fill a jar with hot water. Pour ¼ cup melted butter on top of water. Dip ears of corn in jar.
▶ Roast on grill (page 26).

EASY CORN PUDDING

1 package Jiffy corn bread mix
½ cup (1 stick) butter, melted
3 eggs, beaten
1   16-ounce can whole
    kernel corn, drained
1   16-ounce can cream-style
    corn
1 cup sour cream
1 cup shredded cheese

▶ Preheat oven to 375 degrees.
▶ Mix corn bread mix, butter, eggs, whole kernel and cream-style corn and sour cream in bowl.
▶ Spoon into 1½-quart baking dish. Top with cheese. Bake for 45 minutes.
▶ Yield: 6 servings.

PEAS AND SNOW PEAS

Choose fresh light green pea pods filled with well-developed peas. Store in refrigerator in pods for up to 2 days. Shell peas when ready to cook; discard pods. Two pounds unshelled peas makes 4 servings. Snow peas are eaten pod and all. Choose delicate pods without well-developed peas. Wash pods and remove stem and strings. One pound makes 4 servings.

Stove Top—Place peas in 1 inch boiling water in saucepan; reduce heat. Simmer, covered, for 5 to 8 minutes or until tender; drain.

Microwave—Place peas or snow peas in shallow glass dish with ¼ cup water. Microwave peas, covered, on High for 5 to 8 minutes or until tender. Microwave snow peas on High for 3 to 5 minutes or until tender.

Serving Suggestions
► Serve peas in white sauce (page 71). Add pearl onions, mushrooms or chopped pimento.
► Add snow peas to stir-fried dishes.
► Stuff snow peas with flavored cream cheese or wrap around shrimp for party appetizers.

MINTED ORANGE PEAS

2   10-ounce packages
    frozen peas
2 teaspoons grated orange
    rind
2 teaspoons sugar

Juice of ½ orange
2 tablespoons chopped fresh
    or ½ teaspoon dried mint
Salt to taste

► Cook peas according to directions above; keep warm.
► Combine orange rind, sugar, orange juice, mint and salt in saucepan. Simmer over low heat for 5 minutes.
► Drain peas. Add to sauce. Heat to serving temperature.
► Yields 6 servings.

SNOW PEAS AND TOMATOES

¼ cup chopped onion
2 tablespoons butter
1 pound snow peas
1 tablespoon soy sauce

1 teaspoon oregano
½ teaspoon salt
3 medium tomatoes,
    cut into wedges

► Sauté onion in butter in skillet until transparent. Add snow peas, soy sauce, oregano and salt.
► Stir-fry for 3 minutes or until snow peas are tender-crisp.
► Add tomatoes. Cook, covered, for 1 minute. Spoon into serving dish.
► Yields 4 servings.

POTATOES

There are round potatoes, long potatoes, red potatoes and white potatoes. Choose firm smooth potatoes with shallow eyes. Avoid those with sprouts or patches of green. Store potatoes in a cool dark place. Prepare potatoes in their skins when you can to preserve the nutrients. Scrub the skins well with a vegetable brush. Two pounds of potatoes makes 4 servings.

Stove Top—Cook potatoes in boiling salted water to cover in a saucepan. Allow 30 to 40 minutes for whole potatoes, 20 to 25 minutes for quartered potatoes, 12 to 15 minutes for small new potatoes or chopped potatoes.

Microwave—Pierce skins with fork. Place on paper towel in microwave. Microwave on High for 6 to 9 minutes for 2 potatoes and for 10 to 13 minutes for 4 potatoes; turn once. Let stand for 5 minutes.

Oven—Pierce skins with fork. Bake potatoes at 400 degrees for 45 minutes or until tender. Bake foil-wrapped potatoes at 350 degrees for 1½ hours.

Serving Suggestions
▶ Serve boiled new potatoes with White Sauce (page 71), or with olive oil and garlic salt.
▶ Spoon Cheese Sauce (page 71) over cooked potatoes and broil until potatoes are bubbly.

REAL MASHED POTATOES

8 potatoes, peeled, chopped
½ cup (or more) hot milk

½ cup butter
Salt and pepper to taste

▶ Cook potatoes according to instructions above; drain.
▶ Combine with milk, butter, salt and pepper in mixer bowl; beat until fluffy.
▶ Spoon into serving dish. Garnish with chives, paprika or parsley.
▶ Yields 8 servings.

VARIATIONS

Add 1 or more of the following to real or packaged instant mashed potatoes. Choose the ones you like best.

¼ cup crumbled crisp-fried
  bacon
1½ tablespoons crumbled
  blue cheese
1   4-ounce can chopped
  mushrooms, drained
¾ cup shredded cheese

1 tablespoon chopped red
  or green pepper
1 to 2 tablespoons chives or
  green onions
1 tablespoon chopped
  parsley
¼ teaspoon dillweed

MAKE-AHEAD POTATO CASSEROLE

Prepare in advance, refrigerate up to 24 hours and bring to room temperature before baking.

1 32-ounce package frozen
   hashed brown potatoes
2 cups sour cream
1 10-ounce can condensed
   cream of onion soup

½ cup (1 stick) butter, melted
Salt and pepper to taste
2 cups shredded Cheddar
   cheese

► Preheat oven to 350 degrees.
► Combine potatoes, sour cream, soup, butter and seasonings in bowl. Add half the cheese; mix well.
► Spoon into buttered 9x13-inch baking dish. Sprinkle with remaining cheese. Bake for 1 hour.
► Yields 8 servings.

SCALLOPED POTATOES

6 medium potatoes
1 10-ounce can condensed
   cream of potato soup

½ soup can milk
1 cup shredded Cheddar
   cheese

► Preheat oven to 400 degrees. Peel and slice potatoes. Arrange in greased 1½-quart baking dish.
► Combine soup and milk in bowl. Pour over potatoes.
► Sprinkle with cheese. Bake for 45 minutes or until tender.
► Yields 6 to 8 servings.

TWICE-BAKED POTATOES

Make these potatoes ahead of time and bake the second time just before serving.

4 medium baking potatoes
6 tablespoons butter
⅓ cup milk
2 teaspoons chopped chives

Salt and pepper to taste
2 cups shredded Cheddar
   cheese

► Preheat oven to 350 degrees. Bake potatoes for 1 hour or until tender.
► Cut shallow lengthwise slice from 1 side of potatoes. Scoop out pulp, reserving shells.
► Combine pulp with butter, milk, chives, seasonings and half the cheese. Beat until light and fluffy.
► Spoon pulp into reserved shells. Sprinkle with remaining cheese. Bake for 20 minutes.
► Yields 4 servings.

SPINACH

Choose small leaves that are crisp and fresh. Store in the refrigerator for up to several days. Wash spinach very well under running water when ready to use; discard tough stems. One pound cooked spinach makes 4 servings.

Stove Top—Cook undrained fresh spinach with 2 tablespoons water in covered saucepan over medium heat until steam begins to form. Simmer over low heat for 5 minutes or until tender, stirring occasionally. Drain.

Microwave—Microwave spinach with 2 tablespoons water in covered 3-quart glass bowl on High for 5 to 8 minutes or until tender, stirring once.

Serving Suggestions
► Mix drained cooked spinach with cream sauce (page 71).
► Use spinach for broccoli in Broccoli and Rice Casserole (page 74).
► Combine 3 cups hot cooked spinach mixed with 2 cups sour cream and 1 envelope dry onion soup mix.

POPEYE'S SPECIAL SPINACH

2　10-ounce packages frozen chopped spinach
6 eggs, beaten
2 cups cottage cheese
½ cup (1 stick) butter, sliced
6 tablespoons flour
2 cups shredded Cheddar cheese

► Preheat oven to 350 degrees. Thaw spinach; drain and squeeze dry.
► Combine spinach, eggs, cottage cheese, butter, flour and Cheddar cheese in bowl; mix well.
► Spoon into greased 9x13-inch baking dish. Bake for 1 hour.
► Yields 8 to 10 servings.

SQUASH

The most popular kinds of squash are yellow crookneck and zucchini. Choose firm young squash with glossy skins. Store in refrigerator for up to 2 days. Do not peel squash, just wash and cut off the ends. Two pounds makes 4 servings.

Stove Top—Simmer sliced squash with 2 tablespoons water in covered saucepan or sauté in butter in skillet until tender-crisp.

Microwave—Microwave sliced squash with 2 tablespoons butter in covered glass dish for 3 to 6 minutes or until tender, stirring once.

Serving Suggestions
► Stir-fry squash with onions, mushrooms and tomato. Sprinkle with herbs and seasonings to taste.
► Sprinkle with buttered crumbs or herb-seasoned stuffing mix.

ZUCCHINI SQUARES

4 eggs, beaten
½ cup oil
½ cup grated onion
2 cups grated zucchini
½ cup Bisquick

1 cup shredded Cheddar
  cheese
Garlic powder to taste
½ teaspoon basil
½ teaspoon salt

▶ Preheat oven to 350 degrees. Grease 9x9-inch baking pan.
▶ Combine all 9 ingredients in bowl; mix well. Spoon into prepared pan.
▶ Bake for 30 minutes or until set. Cut into squares.
▶ Yields 9 servings.

CALIFORNIA SQUASH

3 cups sliced squash
1 medium onion, sliced
3 tomatoes, thinly sliced

2 cups Monterey Jack cheese
  with jalapeño peppers
Basil, salt and pepper to taste

▶ Preheat oven to 350 degrees.
▶ Alternate layers of squash, onion, tomatoes, cheese and seasonings in
  1½-quart baking dish. Bake for 30 minutes.
▶ Yields 6 servings.

SWEET POTATOES

Prepare in the same manner as potatoes (page 78).

Serving Suggestions
▶ Serve baked, with butter and salt.
▶ Drizzle slices with canned butterscotch or caramel ice cream topping,
  sprinkle with pecans or walnuts, then bake.

CRUNCHY SWEET POTATO CASSEROLE

3 cups mashed sweet
  potatoes
¾ cup sugar
⅓ cup margarine, softened
⅓ cup milk

1 teaspoon vanilla extract
⅓ cup flour
1 cup packed brown sugar
⅓ cup margarine, softened
½ cup chopped nuts

▶ Preheat oven to 350 degrees.
▶ Combine sweet potatoes, sugar, ⅓ cup margarine, milk and vanilla in
  bowl; beat until smooth. Spoon into 1½-quart baking dish.
▶ Mix flour, brown sugar, ⅓ cup margarine and nuts in bowl until crumbly.
▶ Sprinkle crumb mixture over sweet potatoes. Bake for 30 minutes.
▶ Yields 8 servings.

RICE

Rice is a grain rather than a vegetable. It is served as a side dish or in combination with vegetables and meats. The best white rice is long grain rice. Brown rice has a nuttier flavor and chewier texture and takes longer to cook. Minute rice has been precooked and is ready to eat in 5 minutes. One cup uncooked long grain rice yields 3 cups cooked; brown rice yields 4 cups cooked; and minute rice yields 2 cups cooked.

Stove Top—Add 1 cup long grain rice and 1 teaspoon salt to 2 cups boiling water in saucepan over high heat. Reduce heat. Simmer, covered, over very low heat for 20 minutes. Remove from heat and let stand, covered, for several minutes. Fluff with fork. Cook 1 cup brown rice as above in 2½ cups water for 50 minutes. Stir 1 cup minute rice into 1 cup boiling salted water. Cover and remove from heat. Let stand for 5 minutes and fluff with fork.

Oven—Bring to a boil as above. Bake in a covered casserole at 350 degrees for 25 to 30 minutes for white rice and 1 hour for brown rice.

Serving Suggestions
▶ Substitute chicken broth, beef broth, consommé, tomato juice, vegetable juice or fruit juice for water.
▶ Pack into greased ring mold and invert onto serving plate. Fill with creamed vegetables, chicken or seafood.
▶ Add 1 cup raisins, ½ cup slivered almonds and ½ teaspoon curry powder for curried rice.
▶ Combine with broccoli or spinach for green rice.
▶ Use as a substitute for potatoes.
▶ Combine with vanilla instant pudding and layer with fresh fruit in parfait glasses for a light dessert.

EASY PARTY RICE

1 onion, finely chopped
1　4-ounce can sliced mushrooms, drained
½ cup (1 stick) butter
1 cup long grain rice
1　10-ounce can consommé
1 cup water
Salt and pepper to taste

▶ Preheat oven to 350 degrees.
▶ Sauté onion and mushrooms in butter in saucepan. Add rice, consommé, water, salt and pepper; mix well.
▶ Pour into 1½-quart baking dish. Bake for 1 hour or until liquid is absorbed and rice is tender, stirring occasionally.
▶ Yields 8 servings.

Here's The Beef

Beef

Beef, the all-American meat, has been popular since cowboy days and is still served in some way in most American homes several times each week. While there is an almost endless variety of beef cuts, you do need to know which to buy, as there is a great difference in their tenderness. Stew beef (less tender) will make a very tough shish kabob, for example, while tenderloin is much too tender for a braised (slow cooking) pot roast. Roasting or grilling enhances the flavor of a tender steak or roast. Slow cooking in liquid or marinating for several hours tenderizes less tender cuts of beef. Use our Basic Tenderizing Marinade (page 85).

ROASTING BEEF

Suitable for Roasting	**May Need Tenderizing**
Rib roast	Sirloin tip roast
Rib-eye roast	Bottom round roast
Whole tenderloin	Rump roast

▶ Preheat oven to 325 degrees.
▶ Season the roast with salt and pepper and place fat side up on rack in roasting pan. Insert meat thermometer into thickest part of roast. Do not let thermometer touch bone.
▶ Roast to 140 degrees for rare, 160 degrees for medium or to 170 degrees for well done.

BROILING BEEF

Suitable for Broiling
Club steak
Sirloin steak
T-bone steak
Rib-eye steak

May Need Tenderizing
Flank steak
Chuck steak
Round steak

▶ Preheat oven to broil.
▶ Trim fat from steak, leaving ½ inch. Cut remaining fat at 2-inch intervals to prevent curling. Place on rack over roasting pan.
▶ Broil until browned; turn and brown remaining side.

BASIC TENDERIZING MARINADE

This is a basic marinade for tenderizing roasts and steaks.

1 cup oil
½ cup lemon juice or
 wine vinegar
¼ cup Worcestershire sauce

¾ cup soy sauce
2 cloves of garlic
¼ cup prepared mustard
 (optional)

▶ Combine all 6 ingredients with steak or roast in plastic bag; seal. Place bag in dish.
▶ Marinate in refrigerator for 12 to 48 hours. Turn beef every 6 hours.
▶ Cook according to recipe instructions.
▶ Yields 2¾ cups.

BRAISING BEEF

The following cuts of beef are suitable for braising or slow cooking.

Sirloin tip
Bottom round
Chuck roast
Rump roast

Flank steak
Shoulder roast
Round steak
Stew beef

▶ Preheat oven to 325 to 350 degrees.
▶ Brown the roast, steak or cubed beef in oil in Dutch oven. Spoon off drippings. Add seasonings to taste and 1 cup broth, water or soup; cover Dutch oven tightly.
▶ Bake for several hours or until beef is tender when pierced with fork.
▶ Add carrots, onions and potatoes before baking if desired.
▶ May simmer beef over low heat on stove top instead of baking.

STIR-FRY PEPPER STEAK

1½ pounds flank steak or
   round steak
2 tablespoons cornstarch
2 tablespoons soy sauce
½ teaspoon ginger
2 tablespoons water
3 tablespoons oil

2 green peppers, cut into
   strips
1 onion, coarsely chopped
1½ cups bean sprouts
1 cup small mushrooms,
   cut into halves
4 cups cooked rice

▶ Freeze steak until partially frozen; slice thinly across the grain.
▶ Combine cornstarch, soy sauce, ginger and water in small bowl; blend well; add steak. Marinate for 30 minutes or longer.
▶ Heat oil in skillet or wok. Add vegetables. Stir-fry over medium-high heat until tender-crisp; remove with slotted spoon. Add steak with marinade. Stir-fry until tender.
▶ Stir in vegetables. Heat to serving temperature.
▶ Serve with rice and additional soy sauce.
▶ Yields 6 servings.

LAZY DAY BEEF STEW

1½ pounds lean stew beef
1 onion, chopped
2 tablespoons oil
1   1½-ounce package stew
   seasoning mix
1   16-ounce can tomatoes

2 cups water
3 potatoes, peeled, chopped
1   16-ounce package frozen
   mixed vegetables
Salt and pepper to taste

▶ Brown beef with onion in oil in saucepan, stirring until beef is evenly browned on all sides. Add remaining ingredients; mix well.
▶ Cook over low heat for 2 hours or longer.
▶ Yields 6 servings.

OVEN-BAKED BRISKET

2   10-ounce cans beef
   consommé
1   4-ounce bottle of liquid
   smoke

1   4-ounce bottle of soy sauce
Juice of 1 lemon
1   5 to 7-pound brisket

▶ Preheat oven to 250 degrees.
▶ Combine consommé, liquid smoke, soy sauce and lemon juice in shallow baking dish, mixing well. Add brisket.
▶ Marinate, covered, in refrigerator for 24 to 48 hours, turning occasionally.
▶ Bake, covered, for 4½ to 5 hours or until tender. Slice thinly across the grain; serve with pan juices.
▶ Yields 12 servings.

STEAK BAKE

This recipe may also be prepared using a sirloin tip roast or bone-less chuck roast.

1½ pounds round steak
1   1½-ounce envelope dry
    onion soup mix

1   10-ounce can condensed
    cream of mushroom soup

► Preheat oven to 350 degrees.
► Cut round steak into serving pieces. Place in shallow baking dish.
► Sprinkle dry onion soup mix over steak. Spoon mushroom soup over top. Cover tightly with foil. Bake for 1 hour.
► Yields 5 servings.

CORNED BEEF HASH NESTS

1 tablespoon melted butter
   or margarine

1   16-ounce can
    corned beef hash

► Preheat oven to 350 degrees.
► Brush muffin cups with butter. Pack corned beef hash into muffin cups.
► Bake at 350 degrees until heated through. Remove to serving plate.
► Yields 4 servings.

VARIATIONS

Egg Nests—Make shallow indentation in tops of nests in muffin cups. Break egg carefully into each nest. Bake until eggs are set.

Vegetable Nests—Fill indentations in nests with cooked mixed vegetables. Sprinkle with cheese before baking.

Onion Nests—Fill with canned French-fried onions before baking.

SWISS STEAK

1½ pounds round steak,
   cut into serving pieces
½ cup flour
½ teaspoon dry mustard
½ teaspoon salt

¼ teaspoon pepper
2 tablespoons oil
2 onions, thinly sliced
½ cup chopped green pepper
1   28-ounce can tomatoes

► Trim steak. Combine flour, dry mustard, salt and pepper in bag. Add steaks, shaking to coat well.
► Brown in hot oil in Dutch oven, turning once; drain on paper towel.
► Add onions and green pepper to Dutch oven; cook until onions are trans-parent, stirring frequently. Add steak and tomatoes.
► Cook, covered, over low heat for 1½ hours or until steak is tender.
► Yields 4 servings.

GROUND BEEF

Hamburgers, chopped beefsteak, ground chuck, ground round, it's all the same thing basically—ground beef. Change its shape, and you change its name again—meatballs, meat loaf, Salisbury steak, patties—all still great tasting and America's all-time favorite. You already have your extra special favorites but use your imagination to mix and match ingredients in new ways. Remember that all great recipes had to be invented first.

ALL GROUND BEEF IS NOT CREATED EQUAL

What you see is sometimes not what you get. The law requires that differences be placed on each package you buy. The difference is the percent of fat contained in each type. **Ground beef** contains as much as 30% fat; **Lean Ground Beef** or **Ground Chuck** has no more than 20% fat; and **Extra Lean Ground Beef** or **Ground Round** has no more than 15 % fat. Cost and how you plan to use it help to decide which to choose.

ADD-INS

You can use one or more of these add-ins to invent your own great ground beef recipe. Add your choices to one pound ground beef before shaping.

All-American

2 teaspoons prepared mustard
Chopped chives
2 tablespoons pickle relish
½ envelope dry onion soup mix
3 tablespoons barbecue sauce
Bacon strips, crisp-fried, crumbled
Grated Cheddar cheese

Mexican

½ envelope taco seasoning mix
1½ tablespoons chopped green chilies
2 teaspoons chili powder
3 tablespoons chili sauce

Basic

3 tablespoons grated onion
2 teaspoons Worcestershire sauce
2 teaspoons horseradish

Oriental

2 tablespoons soy sauce
5 teaspoons teriyaki sauce
3 tablespoons chopped water chestnuts

Italian

2 tablespoons Parmesan cheese
Italian seasoning
Chopped olives
¼ teaspoon garlic powder
1 tablespoon chopped basil

French

2 tablespoons crumbled
   blue cheese
2 tablespoons shredded
   Gruyère cheese
3 tablespoons chopped
   scallions

Healthy

1 tablespoon chopped
   parsley
¼ cup wheat germ or bran
¾ cup shredded potato
3 tablespoons chopped nuts
   or pine nuts

SHAPING UP

Now that you've mixed in your seasonings, it's time to decide how to shape it—patties, meatballs or meat loaf. When we think of patties, hamburgers pop into mind. Meatballs are just small round patties and a meat loaf is a large patty cooked and served in a different way, but there's nothing hard about it.

Patties—Can be served in a variety of ways—see the sandwich section (page 51). Just remember that if you plan to freeze ground beef for patties, shape the patties first. Thawed ground beef will not stick together well enough to shape the patties later.

Meatballs—Can be shaped large, small or medium-sized. Here again, use the basic add-ins to suit your taste.

Meat Loaves—Need a little help to hold together well. Just add "fillers" such as bread crumbs, cracker crumbs, sometimes an egg, to help them keep their shape while cooking.

BASIC PATTIES

Shape 1 pound ground beef (with or without add-ins) into 4 patties. Season with salt and pepper after cooking.

Stove Top—Cook in ungreased skillet for 10 minutes or until brown on both sides. Pour off drippings.

Oven—Place on rack in broiler pan. Broil 4 inches from heat source for 10 minutes or to desired degree of doneness, turning once.

Grill—Grill 4 inches from coals for 10 to 15 minutes or to desired degree of doneness, turning once.

BASIC MEATBALLS AND MEAT LOAVES

1 pound ground beef
1 egg, beaten
2 tablespoons grated onion
⅓ cup dry bread crumbs

¼ cup milk
½ teaspoon salt
⅛ teaspoon pepper

► Combine all ingredients and add-ins of your choice in bowl; mix well.
► Shape into meatballs or meat loaf.
► Yields 4 servings.

MEATBALLS

Stove Top—Brown meatballs in 2 tablespoons oil in skillet, turning until evenly browned and cooked through. Drain on paper towel.

Oven—Place meatballs in 9x13-inch baking pan. Bake, uncovered, at 400 degrees for 20 minutes or until brown. Drain.

Microwave—Coat meatballs with 1 envelope dry brown gravy mix. Place in glass baking dish. Microwave, covered with waxed paper, on High for 8 minutes or until cooked through. Drain. Gravy mix adds brown color.

MEAT LOAF

In addition to the Basic Add-Ins, meat loaves can be filled with cheeses or vegetables for a special surprise. Bake at 350 degrees for 50 to 60 minutes, draining if necessary.

ADD-ON SAUCES

Use with 1 pound ground beef shaped into patties, meatballs or meat loaf.

READY-MADE SAUCES

1½ cups barbecue sauce
1½ cups chili sauce

1½ cups spaghetti sauce
2 cans hot dog sauce

DO IT YOURSELF SAUCES

Gravy—1 envelope brown gravy mix, prepared as directed.

Veggie—1 can vegetable soup mixed with ½ cup water.

Mushroom—1 can mushroom soup mixed with ½ cup milk and 1 drained 4-ounce can mushrooms.

Stroganoff—1 cup sour cream with 1 drained 4-ounce can mushrooms.

Onion—1 cup sour cream mixed with ¼ cup milk and ½ envelope dry onion soup mix

Sweet-Sour—1 cup sweet-sour sauce with 1 cup pineapple tidbits.

ADD-UNDERS

Serve ground beef patties, meatballs or meat loaf on one of these delicious "foundations."

Buns, toast, corn bread
Chow mein noodles
Pasta

Hashed brown potatoes
Mashed potatoes
Rice

GROUND BEEF PATTY MEAL IN FOIL

This is an easy 1-step meal.

1½ pounds ground beef
1 envelope brown gravy mix
1   10-ounce package frozen
   mixed vegetables, thawed

1   16-ounce package frozen
   Tater Tots
Salt and pepper to taste

▶ Shape ground beef into 6 patties; place each patty on 12x18-inch piece of heavy-duty foil.
▶ Sprinkle each patty with dry gravy mix, mixed vegetables, Tater Tots, salt and pepper.
▶ Wrap to enclose meal; seal well. Place on baking sheet or grill.
▶ Bake at 400 degrees or grill for 35 minutes.
▶ Yields 6 servings.

PORCUPINES

1 pound ground beef
½ cup uncooked rice
2 tablespoons grated onion
½ teaspoon celery salt
¼ teaspoon garlic salt

¼ teaspoon pepper
2 cups tomato juice
1 teaspoon sugar
1 tablespoon Worcestershire
   sauce

▶ Combine ground beef, rice, onion and seasonings in bowl; mix well.
▶ Shape into 1½-inch balls. Heat remaining ingredients in saucepan.
▶ Yields 4 servings.

Stove Top—Simmer meatballs in tomato sauce in covered saucepan for 45 minutes or to desired consistency.

Oven—Pour hot tomato sauce over meatballs before baking. Bake in 9x9-inch baking dish at 350 degrees for 45 minutes.

Microwave—Microwave meatballs and hot tomato sauce in glass dish on High for 8 minutes.

THE GROUND BEEF SCRAMBLE

There is life after burgers. Ground beef is not always shaped into patties. Many recipes call for ground beef that is cooked until "crumbly," then mixed with other ingredients for a wonderful variety of dishes. Some of your favorites using the Ground Beef Scramble may be found in other sections of this book (check Index). Or you can try 1 of our simple recipes that are made on top of the stove, in the oven, in a Crock•Pot or in the microwave. If you have "added in" and "added on" enough things, you should be well on your way to an easy and exciting meal.

BASIC GROUND BEEF SCRAMBLE

For 1 pound of ground beef.

Stove Top—Cook crumbled ground beef in skillet over medium heat for 10 minutes or until browned, stirring frequently. Drain.

Oven—Bake block of ground beef in baking dish at 350 degrees for 45 minutes or until no longer pink. Drain several times and crumble.

Microwave—Crumble ground beef into plastic colander. Microwave in glass bowl on High for 5 minutes or until no longer pink, stirring twice.

HAMBURGER PANCAKES

3 eggs, separated	1 tablespoon grated onion
½ pound ground beef, scrambled	1 tablespoon minced parsley
	1 teaspoon lemon juice
¼ teaspoon baking powder	Salt and pepper to taste

▶ Beat egg yolks in bowl. Add ground beef, baking powder, onion, parsley, lemon juice, salt and pepper; mix well.
▶ Beat egg whites in bowl until stiff peaks form. Fold gently into the ground beef mixture.
▶ Heat griddle until hot; grease lightly. Drop pancakes by spoonfuls onto griddle. Cook until puffed and brown on both sides.
▶ Serve with creamed vegetables, cheese sauce or mushroom sauce.
▶ Yields 4 servings.

VARIETY SCRAMBLE

This filling can be used in several ways.

1 pound ground beef
½ cup chopped onion
½ cup chopped green pepper
2 cups minute rice
2 cups boiling water

1 28-ounce can tomatoes
Salt and pepper to taste
Chili powder or Italian
  seasoning to taste
  (optional)

► Brown ground beef with onion and green pepper in saucepan, stirring until ground beef is crumbly; drain.
► Combine rice with boiling water in saucepan. Let stand, covered, for 5 minutes. Fluff with fork.
► Add rice, tomatoes and seasonings to ground beef mixture; mix well.
► Yields 4 to 6 servings.

VARIATIONS

Stuffed Green Peppers—Spoon ground beef mixture into green peppers that have been cooked in boiling water for 5 minutes and drained. Bake at 350 degrees for 20 minutes.

Cabbage Rolls—Cook cabbage in boiling water to cover in saucepan until desired number of leaves can be removed. Spoon ground beef mixture onto cabbage leaves; roll to enclose filling. Place in skillet or baking dish. Top with 1 can tomato soup. Simmer or bake at 350 degrees until bubbly.

Stuffed French Loaves—Hollow out small French loaves. Spoon ground beef mixture into centers. Bake at 350 degrees until heated through.

Mexican Stack-Ups—Spoon ground beef mixture over crushed taco chips. Sprinkle with chopped lettuce and tomatoes. Sprinkle with grated cheese and chopped green chilies.

CROCK•POT CHILI

1½ pounds ground beef
½ cup chopped onion
1 clove of garlic, minced
1 16-ounce can tomatoes
1 6-ounce can tomato paste

1 16-ounce can kidney
  beans
1 tablespoon (or more)
  chili powder
Salt and pepper to taste

► Brown ground beef with onion and garlic in skillet, stirring until ground beef is crumbly; drain.
► Combine with remaining ingredients in Crock•Pot; mix well.
► Cook on Low for 6 to 8 hours.
► Garnish servings with shredded Cheddar cheese.
► Yields 4 to 6 servings.

EASY STROGANOFF

1½ pounds ground beef
1 cup chopped onion
1   10-ounce can condensed
   cream of mushroom soup
1 soup can milk

1   3-ounce can sliced
   mushrooms, drained
Salt and pepper to taste
1 cup sour cream
6 cups cooked noodles

► Brown ground beef and onion in skillet, stirring until ground beef is crumbly; drain. Add soup, milk, mushrooms, salt and pepper; mix well.
► Simmer until heated through; stir in sour cream. Serve over noodles.
► Yields 8 servings.

MICROWAVE MEXICAN CASSEROLE

1 pound ground beef
1 can Ro-Tel tomatoes and
   green chilies
1   10-ounce can condensed
   cream of mushroom soup

3 cups crushed tortilla chips
1 cup shredded Cheddar
   cheese

► Microwave ground beef according to Basic Scramble recipe on page 92.
► Add Ro-Tel and soup; mix well. Layer chips, ground beef mixture and cheese ½ at a time in glass casserole.
► Microwave on High for 10 to 12 minutes or until heated through.
► Yields 6 servings.

MEAT AND POTATOES PIE

1 pound ground beef
¼ cup chopped onion
¼ cup chopped green pepper
1   8-ounce can tomato sauce
Salt and pepper to taste
1 unbaked 9-inch pie shell
1 egg, beaten

¼ cup milk
½ teaspoon dry mustard
1 teaspoon Worcestershire
   sauce
2 cups shredded Cheddar
   cheese
3 cups hot mashed potatoes

► Brown ground beef with onion and green pepper in skillet, stirring until ground beef is crumbly; drain.
► Add tomato sauce and seasonings. Spoon into pie shell.
► Combine egg, milk, dry mustard, Worcestershire sauce and cheese in bowl; mix well. Pour over ground beef mixture.
► Bake at 400 degrees for 20 minutes. Spoon potatoes over top.
► Bake for 15 minutes longer or until light brown. Cut into wedges to serve.
► Yields 6 servings.

Chic

Chick

◆ ◆ ◆ ◆ ◆ ◆ ◆ ◆ ◆ ◆ ◆
◆ ◆ ◆ ◆ **Chicken** ◆ ◆ ◆ ◆ ◆

Most live chickens look pretty much alike, but in the supermarket there's a confusing variety. It's in a can, cut up or whole, fresh or frozen. What is it all about? Your choice depends on what you plan to do with it.

First of all, check page 97 to understand the "parts of a chicken." Good advice: buy the chicken already cut up like you want. All chickens can be roasted or stewed whole, then cut into slices or chunks to be eaten or used in cooked casseroles or salads. Always rinse uncooked chicken before preparing. When cooked on the grill, chickens are usually split into halves. When frying, it is cut up into pieces.

BASIC ROASTED CHICKEN

Stuff chicken with Apple-Rice Stuffing or prepared stuffing mix.

► Place whole chicken breast side up on a rack or in a roasting pan; do not cover. Insert a meat thermometer between the thigh and body; do not allow the thermometer tip to touch a bone or the temperature will tell you the chicken is done when it isn't.
► Place in preheated 450-degree oven; reduce temperature to 350 degrees. Roast for about 25 minutes per pound or to 185 to 190 degrees on meat thermometer.
► Baste the chicken every 10 minutes with pan drippings (the juices that cook out of the chicken and collect in the pan) or your favorite sauce.

APPLE-RICE STUFFING FOR ROASTED CHICKEN

1 package long grain
  and wild rice mix
½ cup chopped onion
½ cup chopped celery

2 tablespoons butter
½ cup chopped unpeeled
  apple
½ cup chopped pecans

▶ Cook rice according to package directions.
▶ Sauté onion and celery in butter in saucepan until tender-crisp. Add rice, apple and pecans; mix well.
▶ Spoon rice mixture loosely into cavity of chicken before roasting; tie chicken legs together.
▶ Roast according to directions above, allowing slightly more roasting time per pound.
▶ Yields 6 servings.

PARTS OF A CHICKEN

Chicken pieces, quarters or split halves can be roasted in a 325-degree oven or grilled over medium coals. Cook for about 1 hour or until juices run clear with no trace of pink when pierced with fork. Baste with your favorite sauce, our Basic Vinegar-Based or Tomato-Based Barbecue Sauces (page 21) or try some of the following simple marinades and sauces.

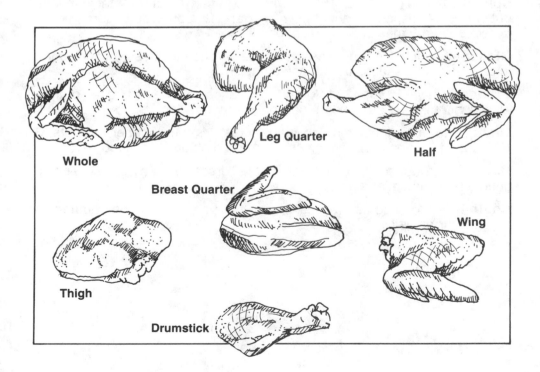

Whole

Leg Quarter

Half

Breast Quarter

Thigh

Wing

Drumstick

MARINADES

Combine all ingredients in shallow dish; mix well. Add chicken; turn to coat well. Marinate in refrigerator for 2 hours or longer. Drain, reserving marinade. Roast chicken as directed on page 96, basting with reserved marinade.

Chili—12-ounce bottle of chili sauce, ½ cup red wine vinegar, 1 tablespoon horseradish, 1 clove of minced garlic, ½ teaspoon salt.

Hawaiian—1 cup pineapple juice, ¼ cup drained crushed pineapple, 2 tablespoons honey, 2 tablespoons soy sauce, 2 teaspoons ginger, 1 teaspoon thyme, seasoned salt and pepper to taste.

Honey—½ cup soy sauce, ½ cup honey, 4 minced green onions, ½ teaspoon ginger.

Lemon—½ cup lemon juice, 1 cup oil, 2 teaspoons onion powder, ½ teaspoon garlic salt, 2 teaspoons basil, 1 teaspoon paprika.

SAUCES

Combine all ingredients in saucepan. Heat until bubbly, mixing well. Brush on chicken. Roast as directed (page 96), basting frequently with sauce.

Spicy Cranberry—16-ounce can whole cranberry sauce, 2 tablespoons butter, 1 tablespoon light brown sugar, 1 tablespoon horseradish, ½ teaspoon dry mustard, ¼ teaspoon allspice.

Ginger—½ cup oil, ¾ cup pineapple juice, ¼ cup molasses, ¼ cup lemon juice, ⅓ cup soy sauce, 1 teaspoon ginger.

Orange-Curry—½ cup (1 stick) butter, 6-ounce can thawed frozen orange juice concentrate, ½ teaspoon (or more) curry powder.

Orange-Walnut—1 cup orange marmalade, ½ cup chopped walnuts, 3 tablespoons lemon juice, 1 tablespoon minced onion, 1 teaspoon salt.

Russian—12-ounce bottle of Russian salad dressing, 1 envelope dry onion soup mix, 6-ounce jar apricot preserves,

Chutney—¼ cup golden raisins, ½ cup boiling water, ½ cup chutney, ½ cup red currant jelly.

BEEFY CHICKEN BAKE

1 large jar dried beef
8 chicken breast filets
1 cup sour cream

1 10-ounce can condensed
cream of mushroom soup

► Preheat oven to 300 degrees.
► Shred dried beef into 9x13-inch baking dish; arrange chicken over beef.
► Mix sour cream and soup in bowl; pour over chicken. Bake for 2 hours.
► Yields 8 servings.

CREOLE CHICKEN AND RICE

4 chicken breasts
Salt and pepper to taste
1 cup uncooked rice
1 cup water
1 8-ounce can tomato sauce

¼ cup chopped green pepper
¼ cup chopped celery
¼ cup chopped onion
⅛ teaspoon thyme

► Preheat oven to 350 degrees.
► Place chicken in 1½-quart baking dish; sprinkle with salt and pepper.
► Combine rice, water, tomato sauce, green pepper, celery, onion and thyme in bowl; mix well.
► Pour over chicken. Bake, covered with foil, for 1 hour.
► Yields 4 servings.

OVEN-FRIED CHICKEN FOR SIX

One of the easiest ways to prepare chicken pieces is to choose one of our coatings and shake and bake.

Parmesan Oven-Fried Chicken—Combine 1 cup dry bread crumbs, ½ cup Parmesan cheese, 1 teaspoon garlic powder, 2 tablespoons parsley flakes and ½ teaspoon salt in paper bag. Dip chicken in ½ cup melted butter. Shake in crumbs until well coated. Arrange chicken in 9x9-inch baking dish; do not allow pieces to touch. Drizzle remaining butter over pieces. Bake in preheated 350-degree oven for 45 minutes.

Bisquick Oven-Fried Chicken—Melt ¼ cup butter in 9x9-inch baking dish in 350-degree oven. Shake chicken in ¾ cup Bisquick in paper bag until coated. Place in prepared baking dish; do not allow pieces to touch. Bake for 30 minutes; turn chicken. Bake for 15 minutes or until tender.

Sesame Oven-Fried Chicken—Combine 1 cup crushed cornflake crumbs, 2 tablespoons sesame seed, ½ teaspoon ginger and 1 teaspoon salt in paper bag. Dip chicken into 1 beaten egg. Shake in crumb mixture to coat well. Arrange chicken in 9x9-inch baking dish; do not allow pieces to touch. Drizzle with ¼ cup melted butter. Bake in preheated 350-degree oven for 45 minutes.

CHICKEN STIR-FRY

4 chicken breast filets,
  cut into strips
¼ cup soy sauce
2 tablespoons oil
1 green pepper, cut into strips
2 stalks celery, sliced
  diagonally
1 cup chopped onion

1 cup sliced mushrooms
1½ cups snow peas
1   7-ounce can sliced water
  chestnuts, drained
½ cup water
2 teaspoons cornstarch
Red pepper to taste
3 cups hot cooked rice

▶ Combine chicken with soy sauce in bowl. Let stand for several minutes.
▶ Heat 1 tablespoon oil in wok or skillet. Stir-fry chicken in oil for 3 to 4 minutes or until light brown; remove chicken with slotted spoon.
▶ Add remaining oil to wok. Add green pepper, celery and onion. Stir-fry until tender-crisp; push vegetables to 1 side of wok.
▶ Stir-fry mushrooms, snow peas and water chestnuts in wok for 2 minutes; reduce heat. Return chicken to wok; mix with all the vegetables.
▶ Mix water, cornstarch and pepper in small bowl; stir into chicken mixture. Cook until thickened, stirring constantly. Serve over rice.
▶ Yields 6 servings.

BASIC STEWED CHICKEN

▶ Place the whole chicken or chicken pieces in enough water to cover in large saucepan. Add salt, pepper, a chopped stalk of celery, a chopped onion and a chopped carrot if desired. Simmer, covered, over medium-low heat until chicken is very tender.
▶ Remove chicken and cool on plate. Save the cooking liquid, now called broth, to strain and use in recipes requiring chicken broth. Freeze chicken broth if you do not plan to use it within 24 hours.
▶ Cool chicken enough to handle. Remove the meat from the bones and slice for sandwiches or chop for recipes needing chopped cooked chicken.

CHICKEN AND DUMPLINGS

1   3-pound chicken or
  3 pounds chicken pieces

4   8-inch flour tortillas,
  torn into small pieces

▶ Cook chicken according to Basic Stewed Chicken Recipe.
▶ Remove and discard chicken bones. Strain broth and discard vegetables. Combine chicken and broth in deep saucepan.
▶ Bring broth to simmering point over low heat. Drop tortilla pieces several at a time into broth. Be sure broth keeps on simmering.
▶ Simmer, covered, for 15 minutes or until tortillas are very tender.
▶ Yields 4 servings.

Note—Try the dumpling recipe on the Bisquick box.

CREAMED CHICKEN

1 4-ounce can sliced mushrooms	¼ cup butter
1 6-ounce can peas and carrots	¼ cup flour
¼ cup chopped onion	Milk
¼ cup chopped celery	2 cups chopped cooked chicken
	Salt and pepper to taste

► Drain mushrooms and peas and carrots, reserving liquid. Sauté mushrooms, onion and celery in butter in saucepan until celery is tender.
► Add flour. Cook for 2 minutes, stirring constantly. Add enough milk to reserved vegetable liquid to measure 2 cups. Stir gradually into vegetables in saucepan.
► Cook until thickened, stirring constantly. Stir in chicken, peas and carrots, salt and pepper. Heat to serving temperature.
► Yields 4 servings.

VARIATIONS

Toast Cups—Press slices of trimmed bread into muffin cups. Bake until crisp and light brown. Fill with creamed chicken.

Patty Shells—Bake frozen puff pastry patty shells according to package directions. Fill with creamed chicken.

English Muffins—Spoon creamed chicken over toasted English muffins.

Pie—Spoon creamed chicken into unbaked 8-inch pie shell. Bake at 350 degrees until crust is brown.

Rice or Noodles—Serve over 4 cups hot cooked rice or noodles.

Biscuit-Topped—Spoon creamed chicken into 8-inch baking dish. Top with refrigerator biscuits. Bake at 400 degrees until biscuits are golden.

CHICKEN AND STUFFING CASSEROLE

4 cups chopped cooked chicken	¾ cup chicken broth
2 tablespoons minced onion	1 package herb-seasoned stuffing mix
1 10-ounce can condensed cream of chicken soup	½ cup (1 stick) butter, melted

► Preheat oven to 350 degrees.
► Cook mixture of chicken, onion, soup and broth in saucepan over low heat just until heated through, stirring constantly.
► Toss stuffing mix with butter in bowl.
► Layer chicken mixture and stuffing mixture ½ at a time in 9x13-inch baking dish. Bake for 20 minutes or until bubbly.
► Yields 8 servings.

KING RANCH CASSEROLE

6 6-inch corn tortillas
3 cups chopped cooked
  chicken
½ cup chopped onion
2 cups shredded Cheddar
  cheese

1 can Ro-Tel tomatoes with
  green chilies
2 teaspoons chili powder
1 teaspoon garlic salt
2 10-ounce condensed
  cream of chicken soup

▶ Preheat oven to 350 degrees.
▶ Line a greased 9x13-inch baking dish with tortillas.
▶ Combine chicken, onion, cheese, Ro-Tel tomatoes, chili powder and garlic salt in bowl; mix well.
▶ Pour over tortillas. Stir soup until creamy; spoon over chicken mixture. Bake for 35 minutes or until bubbly.
▶ Yields 8 servings.

QUICK CHICKEN AND NOODLES ALMONDINE

1 6-ounce package noodles
  almondine
½ cup sour cream

1½ cups chopped cooked
  chicken

▶ Cook noodles according to package directions for stove-top method.
▶ Add sour cream and chicken; mix well. Simmer until heated through.
▶ Yields 4 servings.

EASY CHICKEN DIVAN

2 10-ounce packages
  frozen broccoli spears
3 cups chopped cooked
  chicken
½ cup mayonnaise

1 10-ounce can condensed
  cream of mushroom soup
⅓ cup milk
1 tablespoon lemon juice
1 cup crushed potato chips

▶ Preheat oven to 350 degrees.
▶ Cook broccoli according to package directions; drain. Arrange in 9x13-inch baking dish. Sprinkle chicken over broccoli.
▶ Combine mayonnaise, soup, milk and lemon juice in bowl; mix well. Pour over chicken.
▶ Top casserole with potato chips. Bake for 35 minutes.
▶ Yields 8 servings.

Lotsa
Pasta

◆ ◆ ◆ ◆ ◆ ◆ ◆ ◆ ◆ ◆ ◆ ◆ ◆ ◆

Pasta ◆ ◆ ◆ ◆ ◆ ◆

Pasta comes in lots of sizes and shapes. You already know about spaghetti, macaroni and noodles. But there are dozens more varieties as illustrated above. All are made from the same flour and water dough, except for noodles which also add eggs. Specialty pastas add spinach, tomato, beet juice and herbs for color and flavor.

Remember, pasta is a dried product. When cooked, it absorbs water and doubles in volume. Noodles, however, are the exception. They only increase by about 25% as they cook, so the amount you cook should be fairly close to the amount of cooked noodles you will need.

Cooking pasta is very easy, depending mostly on the degree of tenderness which you prefer. The average cooking time is 8 to 10 minutes, but you should check the instructions on the package. Many recipes suggest cooking pasta *al dente*. This is the stage when the pasta becomes tender but is still a little bit chewy. Remember that pasta which will be added to other ingredients and then cooked longer should be precooked only a short time. Drain pasta immediately and rinse. If it remains in its cooking liquid, it will become gummy.

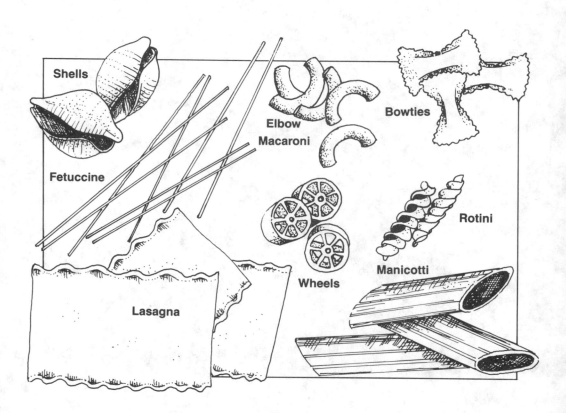

Shells

Elbow Macaroni

Bowties

Fetuccine

Rotini

Wheels

Manicotti

Lasagna

BASIC PASTA

There are so many ways of serving pasta, as a side dish, mixed with meats, vegetables and sauces, or even in salads. Here again is your chance to invent new combinations. For instance, try using one of the unusual sizes and shapes of pasta instead of macaroni. Sauces add variety, too. Use a different cheese with the macaroni or two kinds—be creative and have fun.

6 quarts water   1   16-ounce package pasta
1 (or more) tablespoons salt

▶ Bring water to a boil over high heat in large saucepan. Add salt to taste.
▶ Add pasta gradually so water does not stop boiling. Hold spaghetti verti-
  cally in boiling water until ends soften. Press spaghetti down, coiling it
  around until it is completely submerged.
▶ Stir pasta frequently as it cooks to prevent sticking. Reduce heat slightly
  if saucepan appears about to boil over.
▶ Cook pasta to desired degree of tenderness.
▶ Drain pasta in colander and serve immediately.
▶ Yields 4 to 6 servings.

STIR-INS FOR PASTA

Simple stir-ins are the easiest way to add variety to your pasta. These are limited only by your ingenuity and amounts can vary with your personal taste.

Commercial Spaghetti Sauce—Stir a 28-ounce jar of heated commercial spaghetti sauce into Basic Pasta.

Herbs—Stir any combination of your favorite herbs such as chopped pars-ley, chopped chives, basil, thyme, oregano or Italian seasoning mix and ¼ cup melted butter into Basic Pasta.

Sautéed Nuts—Lightly brown 1 cup slivered almonds or coarsely chopped walnuts in ¼ cup butter in skillet. Stir into Basic Pasta.

Easy Fettucini Alfredo—Add 1½ cups Parmesan cheese, 2 sticks of but-ter and 1 cup half and half, ⅓ at a time, to Basic Pasta fettuccini, stirring constantly over low heat.

Easy Primavera—Stir one 16-ounce package cooked frozen Italian vege-tables and ⅓ cup melted butter into Basic Pasta.

Sour Cream—Stir 1 cup sour cream, ⅓ cup mayonnaise, 2 tablespoons lemon juice and seasonings and herbs to taste into Basic Pasta.

Tangy—Stir 1 envelope dry Italian salad dressing mix, ¾ cup cream, ½ cup butter and ½ cup Parmesan cheese into Basic Pasta.

EASY BEEFED-UP SPAGHETTI SAUCE

This recipe makes commercial spaghetti sauce taste as if it has been cooking all day.

1 pound ground beef
1 28-ounce jar spaghetti
   sauce

1 4-ounce can sliced
   mushrooms, drained
Basic Pasta (page 105)

▶ Brown ground beef over medium heat in a skillet, stirring until beef is crumbly; pour off pan drippings (see page 92).
▶ Add spaghetti sauce and mushrooms; mix well. Simmer over low heat for 10 minutes.
▶ Pour over Basic Pasta in serving bowl; serve with Parmesan cheese.
▶ Yields 4 to 6 servings.

VARIATIONS

Easy Meatballs and Spaghetti—Prepare Meatballs (page 90), and add to one 28-ounce jar spaghetti sauce. Proceed as directed above.

Easy Sausage Spaghetti Sauce—Substitute 1 pound sliced Italian sausage links for ground beef. Proceed as directed above.

HOMEMADE SPAGHETTI SAUCE

This recipe takes a little longer but is no more difficult. Try the suggestions for variety.

1 clove of garlic, minced
1 medium onion, chopped
2 tablespoons olive oil
2 16-ounce cans whole
   tomatoes
1 6-ounce can tomato paste

1 teaspoon basil
1 teaspoon oregano
1 bay leaf
1 teaspoon salt
½ teaspoon pepper
Basic Pasta (page 105)

▶ Cook garlic and onion in olive oil in large saucepan over medium heat, stirring constantly.
▶ Add tomatoes, tomato paste, basil, oregano, bay leaf, salt and pepper; mix well. Reduce heat; simmer, covered, over low heat for 45 minutes or until thickened to desired consistency. Remove bay leaf.
▶ Pour over Basic Pasta in serving bowl. Serve with Parmesan cheese.
▶ Yields 4 to 6 servings.

VARIATIONS

Homemade Spaghetti Sauce with Meat—Brown 1 pound ground beef with garlic and onion and drain excess drippings. Proceed as directed above.

Homemade Spaghetti Sauce with Shrimp—Add 1 pound frozen peeled shrimp to sauce 10 minutes before serving. Simmer for 8 to 10 minutes. Proceed as directed above.

EASY CHICKEN TETRAZZINI

1 10-ounce can condensed cream of chicken soup
1 6-ounce can evaporated milk
1 3-ounce can sliced mushrooms, undrained
2 tablespoons butter
2 tablespoons lemon juice
2 tablespoons Parmesan cheese
2 6-ounce cans chunk chicken
Basic Pasta (page 105)

► Combine soup, evaporated milk, mushrooms with liquid, butter, lemon juice and Parmesan cheese in saucepan; mix well.
► Break up chicken with a fork; add to sauce. Heat until mixture is bubbly.
► Pour chicken mixture over Basic Pasta in serving bowl. Serve with additional Parmesan cheese.
► Yields 4 to 6 servings.

STRAW AND HAY

The name of this dish refers to the colors of the pasta.

8 ounces fettuccini
8 ounces green fettuccini
1¼ cups cream
2 cups cooked green peas
1 cup chopped smoked ham
½ cup Parmesan cheese
¼ teaspoon salt
¼ teaspoon pepper

► Cook fettuccini according to directions for Basic Pasta.
► Heat cream just to the simmering point in saucepan. Stir in peas, ham, Parmesan cheese, salt and pepper. Simmer over low heat for 5 minutes.
► Pour sauce over hot fettuccini in serving bowl; toss gently. Serve with additional Parmesan cheese.
► Yields 4 to 6 servings.

PIZZA PASTA

¼ cup olive oil
1 large onion, thinly sliced
2 green peppers, sliced
8 ounces thinly sliced pepperoni
2 cloves of garlic, minced
1 15-ounce can tomatoes
1 teaspoon oregano
½ teaspoon salt
Basic Pasta (page 105)

► Heat olive oil in skillet over medium heat. Add onion, green peppers, pepperoni and garlic. Cook for 5 minutes, stirring constantly.
► Mix in tomatoes, oregano and salt. Cook, covered, for 5 minutes; stir several times. Remove cover; cook for 5 minutes until sauce thickens slightly.
► Pour over Basic Pasta in serving bowl. Serve with Parmesan cheese.
► Yields 4 to 6 servings.

MACARONI AND CHEESE

1   16-ounce package
    macaroni
2 tablespoons butter
2 cups shredded sharp
    Cheddar cheese

¾ teaspoon salt
¼ teaspoon pepper
2 eggs, beaten
3 cups milk

► Cook macaroni according to instructions for Basic Pasta (page 105).
► Combine butter, cheese, salt and pepper with hot drained macaroni in bowl; mix well. Pour into greased 1½-quart casserole.
► Beat eggs and milk in small bowl until well mixed. Pour over macaroni.
► Bake at 350 degrees for 40 to 50 minutes or until macaroni is set and golden brown on top.
► Yields 6 to 8 servings.

EASY LASAGNA

9 lasagna noodles
1   8-ounce carton small-curd
    cottage cheese
2 eggs, beaten
1 cup Parmesan cheese

3 cups shredded mozzarella
    cheese
1 recipe Easy Beefed-Up
    Spaghetti Sauce (page 106)

► Cook lasagna noodles according to instructions for Basic Pasta (page 105). Rinse and drain noodles.
► Mix cottage cheese and eggs in small bowl. Mix Parmesan cheese and mozzarella cheese in medium bowl.
► Spread a small amount of Spaghetti Sauce in bottom of 9x13-inch baking dish. Arrange 3 noodles in dish. Layer Spaghetti Sauce, cottage cheese mixture and mozzarella cheese mixture ⅓ at a time over noodles.
► Bake at 350 degrees for 45 minutes or until bubbly. Let stand for 10 minutes. Cut into squares.
► Yields 6 servings.

VARIATION

Pinwheel Lasagna—Spread cottage cheese mixture on each noodle. Roll into pinwheel. Place in baking dish. Spoon Spaghetti Sauce over top. Sprinkle with mozzarella cheese. Bake as above.

MICROWAVE ONE-STEP LASAGNA

This time-saving lasagna uses noodles which are not cooked before the casserole is assembled.

1 pound ground beef
1   32-ounce jar spaghetti
   sauce
½ cup water
1 teaspoon salt
8 ounces uncooked lasagna
   noodles

2 cups cottage cheese
3 cups shredded mozzarella
   cheese
½ cup Parmesan cheese

▶ Crumble ground beef into glass dish. Microwave on High for 5 to 6 minutes or until no longer pink; drain.
▶ Stir in spaghetti sauce, water and salt. Microwave, covered, on High for 5 minutes or until heated through.
▶ Layer ⅓ of the sauce, ½ of the noodles, ½ of the cottage cheese and ½ of the mozzarella cheese in 9x13-inch glass casserole.
▶ Repeat layers. Top with remaining sauce and Parmesan cheese. Wrap tightly with plastic wrap.
▶ Microwave on High for 30 minutes or until noodles are tender. Let stand for 5 minutes before serving.
▶ Yields 6 servings.

ONE-STEP BAKED SPAGHETTI

The spaghetti in this recipe is cooked in the oven.

1 recipe Easy Beefed-Up
   Spaghetti Sauce (page 106)
   or Homemade Spaghetti
   Sauce with Meat (page 106)

8 ounces uncooked spaghetti,
   broken
4 cups tomato juice

▶ Combine Spaghetti Sauce, spaghetti and tomato juice in bowl; mix well. Pour into deep baking dish.
▶ Bake at 350 degrees for 1 hour or until spaghetti is tender and liquid is absorbed. Stir occasionally. Serve with Parmesan cheese.
▶ Yields 4 to 6 servings.

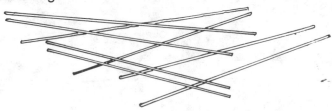

STUFFED PASTA

20 jumbo shells or
   16 manicotti shells
2 cups ricotta cheese
2 cups shredded mozzarella
   cheese
¼ cup chopped parsley
1 egg, beaten

1 teaspoon salt
½ teaspoon pepper
1 recipe Easy Beefed Up
   Spaghetti Sauce or Easy
   Sausage Spaghetti Sauce
   (page 106)
½ cup Parmesan cheese

▶ Cook jumbo shells or manicotti shells according to instructions for Basic Pasta; rinse and drain well.
▶ Combine ricotta cheese, mozzarella cheese, parsley, egg, salt and pepper in bowl; mix well. Stuff into shells.
▶ Spoon half the Spaghetti Sauce into 9x13-inch baking dish. Arrange the stuffed shells in dish. Top with remaining sauce and Parmesan cheese.
▶ Bake at 375 degrees for 30 minutes or until bubbly.
▶ Yields 6 servings.

VARIATION

Spinach Filling—Combine thawed and drained 10-ounce package frozen chopped spinach, ⅓ cup Parmesan cheese, 2 egg yolks, 1 tablespoon softened butter, ¼ teaspoon salt, ⅛ teaspoon pepper and ⅛ teaspoon nutmeg; stuff into shells as above.

TALIARINI

8 ounces noodles, cooked
1   10-ounce can condensed
   cream of mushroom soup
2 to 3 cups spaghetti sauce
1 cup drained whole kernel
   corn

½ cup sliced black olives,
   (optional)
3 cups shredded Cheddar
   cheese
2 cups crushed corn chips

▶ Mix hot cooked noodles with undiluted soup in bowl.
▶ Alternate layers of noodles, spaghetti sauce, corn, olives and cheese in 9x13-inch baking dish, ending with cheese. Top with corn chips.
▶ Bake at 350 degrees until bubbly.
▶ Yields 6 servings.

The
Bun
Warmer

Breads

Bread is our most basic food. In fact, the first recipes invented were probably for a sun-baked loaf. Just stir together a few basic ingredients and bake—the results will smell wonderful and taste delicious. Our breads range from easy—making use of mixes and refrigerator or frozen dough—to mix-your-own quick and yeast breads. Quick breads, including muffins, biscuits and loaves, are easy to mix, require no kneading and rise while baking in the oven. Yeast breads require a rising time for the yeast to work but can be shaped according to your whim. Try them all. Soon you will be a master of bread making.

MUFFINS

Muffins are one of the easiest and most delicious breads to make. There is usually only one bowl to clean up—if you use paper cupcake liners in the muffin cups. The method is simple. A perfect muffin is golden brown and rounded on top.

▶ Combine the dry ingredients in a bowl.
▶ Add a mixture of the liquid ingredients.
▶ Mix with fork just until mixture is moistened.
▶ Stir in nuts or fruit. Fill paper-lined muffin cups ⅔ full.
▶ Bake on center rack of preheated oven until golden brown.

DESIGNER MUFFINS

▶ Start easy with packaged muffin mixes.
▶ Combine 2 different flavors of 6-ounce packages of muffin mix with the liquid required for both packages.
▶ Prepare and bake using the package directions.
▶ Some interesting combinations are cinnamon-apple and bran, blueberry and corn, cranberry-orange and strawberry.

QUICK CORN MUFFINS

Start with a mix but add a few other ingredients for special muffins the quick and easy way.

1 6-ounce package corn muffin mix	½ cup sour cream or yogurt
1 8-ounce can cream-style corn	¼ cup oil
	1 egg

▶ Preheat oven to 375 degrees.
▶ Combine muffin mix, corn, sour cream, oil and egg in bowl; mix well.
▶ Grease 12 muffin cups with shortening. Fill each cup ⅔ full with batter.
▶ Bake on the center rack of preheated oven for 20 minutes or until golden.
▶ Yields 1 dozen muffins.

EVEREADY BRAN MUFFINS

Try making up a big batch of muffin batter to keep in a covered container in the refrigerator for weeks. Whenever you're hungry for muffins just dip out enough to fill muffin cups ⅔ full. Do not stir the batter again!

1 15-ounce package Raisin Bran cereal	1 tablespoon cinnamon
3 cups sugar	2 teaspoons salt
5 cups flour	4 eggs
5 teaspoons soda	1 cup oil
	4 cups buttermilk

▶ Preheat oven to 400 degrees.
▶ Combine cereal, sugar, flour, soda, cinnamon and salt in a very large bowl. Mix with spoon until ingredients are combined.
▶ Mix eggs, oil and buttermilk in bowl with fork until ingredients are blended. Add to the dry ingredients. Stir until ingredients are moistened.
▶ Line as many muffin cups as you need with cupcake liners or grease with shortening. Fill each cup ⅔ full.
▶ Bake for 15 to 20 minutes or until muffins test done.
▶ Store remaining batter, covered, in refrigerator for up to 4 weeks.
▶ Yields 5 dozen muffins.

MUFFINS-YOUR WAY

Make these muffins with all your favorite ingredients. Start with the basics of flour, baking powder, eggs and oil. Add your choice of the rest for muffins any way you like them.

1 cup flour
Choice Number 1: (Choose 1)
   1 cup all-purpose flour,
   whole wheat flour, bran,
   oats or cornmeal
2 teaspoons baking powder
1 egg
¼ cup oil

Choice Number 2: (Choose 1)
   ¼ cup sugar, honey,
   molasses or maple syrup
Choice Number 3: (Choose 1)
   1 cup milk, buttermilk, yogurt
   or fruit juice
Choice Number 4: (Choose 1)
   ½ cup nuts, sunflower seed,
   blueberries or coconut

▶ Preheat oven to 400 degrees.
▶ Combine 1 cup flour, 1 ingredient from Choice Number 1 and baking powder in bowl. Mix until ingredients are combined.
▶ Mix egg, oil and 1 ingredient from Choice Number 2 and 1 from Choice Number 3 in small bowl. Mix with fork until ingredients are blended.
▶ Add liquid mixture to dry ingredients. Mix with fork just until ingredients are moistened. Add 1 ingredient from Choice Number 4.
▶ Line 12 muffin cups with cupcake liners or grease with shortening. Fill each cup ⅔ full.
▶ Bake for 20 minutes or until toothpick inserted in center of 1 muffin comes out clean.
▶ Yield: 1 dozen muffins.

POPOVERS

Popovers look like muffins but are made with a thinner batter. They need to be served hot out of the oven. Don't peek while popovers are baking!

3 eggs
1 cup milk
3 tablespoons melted butter
   or margarine

1 cup flour
½ teaspoon salt

▶ Preheat oven to 375 degrees.
▶ Combine eggs, milk and melted butter in mixer bowl. Beat with electric mixer at low speed until ingredients are blended.
▶ Add flour and salt. Beat until ingredients are blended.
▶ Grease muffin cups or custard cups with shortening. Fill ¾ full with batter.
▶ Bake for 50 minutes. Cut slit in each popover to allow steam to escape. Serve immediately.
▶ Yields 8 popovers.

BISCUITS

Biscuits are light and fluffy, hot and delicious breads which can be made as easily as opening a can of refrigerator biscuits or stirring up a batch of your own. None of these recipes is hard, and you'll love the results for breakfast, lunch, supper or any time.

QUICK HERBED BISCUITS

Pep up refrigerator biscuits by adding easy ingredients to the baking pan they're cooked in. Use our suggestions or other favorite herb mixtures such as Italian seasoning.

¼ cup (½ stick) butter or margarine, softened
¾ teaspoon parsley flakes
½ teaspoon dillweed
1 tablespoon onion flakes
1   10-count can refrigerator biscuits
1 tablespoon Parmesan cheese

▶ Preheat oven to 425 degrees.
▶ Spread butter or margarine in a 9-inch square baking pan. Sprinkle parsley flakes, dillweed and onion flakes over bottom of buttered pan.
▶ Separate biscuits. Place in prepared pan. Sprinkle biscuits with Parmesan cheese.
▶ Bake in preheated oven for 12 to 15 minutes or until biscuits are golden.
▶ Yields 10 biscuits.

MAYONNAISE BISCUITS

Use self-rising flour to make these easy muffin-cup biscuits.

1 cup self-rising flour or Bisquick
½ cup milk
3 tablespoons mayonnaise

▶ Preheat oven to 425 degrees.
▶ Combine flour, milk and mayonnaise in mixer bowl. Mix with fork until ingredients are blended.
▶ Grease 6 muffin cups with shortening. Spoon dough into cups.
▶ Bake in preheated oven for 15 minutes or until golden brown. Serve hot.
▶ Yields 6 biscuits.

SOUR CREAM BISCUITS

Stir ½ cup sour cream and ¼ cup melted butter into 1 cup self-rising flour. Prepare and bake as above.

DROP BISCUITS

Dropping biscuit dough from a spoon saves time and clean-up.

2 cups sifted flour
4 teaspoons baking powder
½ teaspoon salt

¼ cup shortening
¾ cup milk

- ► Preheat oven to 450 degrees.
- ► Sift flour, baking powder and salt into bowl.
- ► Cut in shortening with pastry blender or 2 knives until mixture is crumbly and resembles cornmeal.
- ► Add milk ¼ cup at a time, stirring mixture with fork after each addition.
- ► Drop by tablespoonfuls onto ungreased baking sheet.
- ► Bake in preheated oven for 10 to 12 minutes or until golden brown. Serve hot with butter and jam.
- ► Yields 1 dozen biscuits.

CUT-OUT BISCUITS

- ► Reduce milk to ½ cup.
- ► Pat dough out on a floured surface to ½ to 1-inch thickness. (Thin biscuits will be crispier) Cut out with 2-inch biscuit cutter.
- ► Place biscuits 2 inches apart on baking sheet for crisp biscuits or touching each other for lighter, higher biscuits.
- ► Bake at 450 degrees for 10 minutes or until golden.

QUICK LOAVES

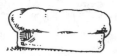

Loaves of bread are impressive whether made for your family or for gifts. Ours are easy, fun to make and great for breakfast, sandwiches, snacks or even dessert.

SPICY APPLESAUCE BREAD

1 cup applesauce
1   17-ounce package yellow
   cake mix
½ teaspoon cinnamon

1   4-ounce package vanilla
   instant pudding mix
½ teaspoon nutmeg
½ cup raisins

- ► Preheat oven to 350 degrees. Grease 2 small (5x7-inch) loaf pans.
- ► Combine applesauce, dry cake mix, cinnamon, dry pudding mix and nutmeg in mixer bowl.
- ► Beat at high speed for 4 minutes. Fold in raisins. Pour into pans.
- ► Bake for 35 minutes or until toothpick inserted in center comes out clean. Cool in pans for 15 minutes. Remove to wire rack to cool completely.
- ► Yields 2 loaves.

QUICK BANANA BREAD

⅓ cup oil
1½ cups mashed ripe
  bananas
3 eggs

½ teaspoon vanilla extract
2⅓ cups Bisquick
1 cup sugar
½ cup chopped pecans

► Preheat oven to 350 degrees. Grease bottom of 5x9-inch loaf pan.
► Combine oil, bananas, eggs, vanilla, Bisquick and sugar in mixer bowl. Beat at high speed for 30 seconds. Fold in pecans. Pour into pan.
► Bake for 55 minutes or until toothpick inserted in center comes out clean. Cool in pan for 5 minutes. Remove to wire rack to cool completely.
► Yields 1 loaf.

CHEDDAR-PECAN BREAD

¾ cup Bisquick
1½ cups shredded sharp
  Cheddar cheese
1 egg, beaten

1 cup evaporated milk
½ cup water
½ cup chopped pecans

► Preheat oven to 350 degrees. Grease 5x9-inch loaf pan.
► Combine Bisquick, cheese, egg, evaporated milk and water in bowl. Mix well with fork. Pour into prepared pan.
► Bake for 55 minutes or until toothpick inserted in center comes out clean. Cool in pan for 10 minutes. Remove to wire rack to cool completely.
► Yields 1 loaf.

STRAWBERRY-BANANA BREAD

2 eggs
1 cup mashed ripe bananas
3 tablespoons milk

2 6-ounce packages
  strawberry muffin mix
1 cup chopped walnuts

► Preheat oven to 375 degrees. Grease 5x9-inch loaf pan.
► Beat eggs in bowl. Add bananas, milk, muffin mix and walnuts. Stir just until moistened.
► Pour batter into prepared loaf pan.
► Bake for 40 to 45 minutes or until bread tests done.
► Cool bread in pan for 10 minutes. Remove to wire rack to cool completely.
► Yields 1 loaf.

YEAST BREADS

Breads made with yeast have a flavor and aroma that cannot be matched. From dressed up breads bought at the bakery to loaves and rolls you make from scratch, these recipes are delicious.

CREOLE BREAD

1 16-ounce loaf French bread
½ cup (1 stick) butter or margarine, softened

2 teaspoons garlic powder
1 teaspoon pepper
2 tablespoons Parmesan cheese

▶ Preheat oven to broil. Split loaf lengthwise into 2 halves.
▶ Mix butter, garlic powder, pepper and cheese in small bowl. Spread on cut sides of loaf. Place buttered sides up on baking sheet.
▶ Broil for 2 minutes or until light brown. Cut into serving-sized pieces.
▶ Yields 8 servings.

ZESTY FRENCH LOAVES

2 8-ounce loaves brown and serve French bread
3 ounces cream cheese with chives, softened

2 tablespoons butter, softened
1 tablespoon horseradish

▶ Preheat oven to 400 degrees. Line baking sheet with foil.
▶ Slice bread ½ inch thick to but not quite through bottom.
▶ Combine cream cheese, butter and horseradish in small bowl; mix well. Spread between slices. Place on baking sheet.
▶ Bake for 12 to 15 minutes or until loaves are brown.
▶ Yields 2 loaves.

CONFETTI BREAD

1 16-ounce package frozen roll dough
1 cup chopped green pepper
1 cup chopped onion

1 cup melted butter or margarine
¼ cup real bacon bits
½ cup Parmesan cheese

▶ Preheat oven to 375 degrees. Thaw rolls.
▶ Sauté green pepper and onion in butter in skillet until tender. Add rolls, bacon bits and cheese; mix well. Spoon into bundt pan. Let rise for 1 hour or until doubled in bulk.
▶ Bake for 30 minutes or until brown. Invert onto serving plate. Pull apart or slice to serve.
▶ Yields 1 loaf.

RICH BATTER BREAD

1 package dry yeast
½ cup warm (110-115 degree) water
⅛ teaspoon ginger
3 tablespoons sugar

2 tablespoons oil
1 12-ounce can evaporated milk
1 teaspoon salt
4 to 4½ cups flour

► Preheat oven to 350 degrees.
► Grease 2-pound coffee can or 2-quart casserole.
► Dissolve yeast in ½ cup warm water in mixer bowl. Water should be 110 to 115 degrees on candy thermometer, just warm to the touch.
► Add ginger and 1 tablespoon sugar. Let stand for 15 minutes.
► Stir in remaining 2 tablespoons sugar, oil, milk and salt.
► Add 3 cups flour, 1 cup at a time, beating at low speed after each addition. Stir in enough remaining flour to make heavy sticky dough.
► Spoon into coffee can or casserole. Let rise, covered, in warm place for 1 hour or until dough reaches top of can or casserole.
► Bake bread for 60 minutes or until brown. Cool in can or casserole on wire rack for 5 minutes. Remove bread from can or casserole.
► Yields 1 loaf.

PEPPERONI BREAD

1 8-ounce loaf frozen bread dough, thawed
¼ cup pizza sauce

1 cup grated mozzarella cheese
4 ounces sliced pepperoni

► Preheat oven to 350 degrees.
► Roll bread dough into rectangle 1 inch thick on floured surface.
► Spread pizza sauce over dough. Sprinkle with cheese and pepperoni. Roll as for jelly roll. Press edge and ends to seal. Place on baking pan. Cut slits in top.
► Bake for 20 minutes or until brown. Let stand for 5 minutes. Cut into slices.
► Yields 1 loaf.

BATTER ROLLS

1 package dry yeast
¾ cup warm (110-115 degree) water

⅓ cup sugar
2 cups Bisquick
1 egg, beaten

► Preheat oven to 400 degrees. Grease 12 muffin cups.
► Dissolve yeast in ¾ cup warm water in bowl. Let stand for 5 minutes.
► Combine sugar and Bisquick in bowl. Add yeast; mix well. Add egg; mix well. Spoon into prepared muffin cups.
► Bake for 15 minutes or until brown. Serve hot.
► Yields 1 dozen.

HOMEMADE BREAD

1 package dry yeast	2 cups milk
3 tablespoons sugar	3 tablespoons butter
2 teaspoons salt	5¾ to 6½ cups flour
2 cups flour	1 tablespoon butter

▶ Preheat oven to 400 degrees.
▶ Combine yeast, sugar, salt and 2 cups flour in mixer bowl.
▶ Heat milk and 3 tablespoons butter in saucepan until very warm, 120 to 130 degrees on candy thermometer. Blend with yeast mixture gradually, beating at low speed. Beat at medium speed for 2 minutes.
▶ Stir in ¾ cup flour. Beat at medium speed for 2 minutes longer. Add 3 cups flour. Mix well with spoon.
▶ Knead dough on floured surface for 10 minutes or until smooth and elastic. Place dough in bowl greased with 1 tablespoon butter; turn dough to grease surface. Cover with clean dish cloth. Place in warm place.
▶ Let rise for 1 hour or until indentation remains when fingers are pressed ½ inch into dough. Divide into 2 portions on floured surface; shape each into oblong roll.
▶ Place each roll in greased 5x9-inch baking pan. Cover each with towel. Let rise for 1 hour or until doubled in bulk.
▶ Bake bread for 25 to 30 minutes or until loaves are brown and sound hollow when tapped. Remove from pans. Cool on wire rack.
▶ Yields 2 loaves.

SHAPING BREAD

Frozen roll or bread dough or yeast bread dough may be shaped into many varieties of rolls.

Braids—Divide dough into 6 portions. Roll each portion into long rope. Place 3 ropes together; braid loosely. Place on greased baking sheet.

Bread Sticks—Roll into 10-inch ropes. Coat with melted butter. Sprinkle with garlic salt. Place on greased baking sheet.

Clover Leaf—Place 3 small balls of dough together in greased muffin cups.

Crescents—Roll dough on lightly floured surface into 9-inch circle. Cut into 12 wedges. Brush with melted butter. Roll each wedge up from wide end. Curve into crescents. Place on greased baking sheet.

Parker House—Roll dough ½-inch thick on lightly floured surface. Cut with biscuit cutter. Brush with melted butter. Fold rolls in half. Brush with melted butter. Place in greased baking pan.

Sweet Rolls—Roll dough into rectangle. Brush with melted butter. Sprinkle with cinnamon-sugar and nuts. Roll as for jelly roll. Cut into slices. Place in greased baking pan.

Let
Them
Eat Cake

♦ ♦ ♦ ♦ ♦ ♦ ♦ ♦ ♦ ♦ ♦ ♦

♦ ♦ ♦ ♦ **Cakes** ♦ ♦ ♦ ♦ ♦ ♦

A cake makes any occasion special. One of the easiest and most versatile desserts, cakes are perfect for birthdays, parties, potluck suppers or dinners at home. With our recipes you can make bakery cakes into special treats, add extras to cake mixes for fast specialties or stir up several cakes from scratch—just like grandmother did.

MAKING A CAKE

Cake Pans—Cakes may be baked in various pan sizes according to the occasion. A basic cake mix or cake recipe may be baked in two 8-inch square or two 9-inch round layer cake pans, a 9x13-inch cake pan, a bundt pan, or 24 cupcakes.

Pan Preparation—In order to remove layers easily, grease bottoms and sides of cake pans with solid unsalted shortening. Sprinkle with a small amount of flour; shake to coat surface and shake out excess flour.

Baking—Bake the cakes on center rack of oven. If using glass cake pans or bundt pan coated with colored enamel, decrease baking temperature by 25 degrees. Cakes baked in various cake pans require different baking times. Cake layers require about 20 minutes, while bundt cakes may take 40 minutes and cupcakes 15 minutes.

Testing—To ensure perfect cakes, test the cake before removing from oven. A toothpick inserted in center should come out clean and dry and the sides of the cake should pull slightly from sides of pans.

TOPPING IT OFF

Start with a bakery cake or a plain cake mix cake. Add one of our special frostings instead of a canned icing. You won't believe the difference—and neither will your friends.

CHOCOLATE FROSTED ANGEL CAKE

8-ounces milk chocolate
16 ounces whipped topping

1 cup chopped almonds
1 large angel food cake

▶ Melt chocolate in top of double boiler over hot water. Cool. Fold gently into whipped topping. Fold in almonds.
▶ Split cake in half. Spread chocolate mixture between layers. Frost cake with remaining mixture. Store in refrigerator.
▶ Yields 8 servings.

VARIATIONS

Toffee—Fold ½ cup crushed Heath bars into chocolate mixture.

Strawberry—Fold 2 cups sliced fresh strawberries into whipped topping instead of chocolate.

FAST AND FANCY POUND CAKE

1 6-ounce package vanilla
   pudding and pie filling mix
   (not instant)
2½ cups milk
1 16-ounce pound cake

1 8-ounce jar apricot jam
1 16-ounce container whipped
   topping
1 cup flaked coconut

▶ Prepare pie filling according to package directions using 2½ cups milk. Cool to room temperature.
▶ Split cake into 4 layers. Spread jam and pudding between layers. Place on cake plate.
▶ Frost cake with whipped topping. Sprinkle with coconut. Refrigerate until serving time.
▶ Yields 10 servings.

BROILED FROSTING

½ cup melted butter
1 cup packed light brown
   sugar
½ cup evaporated milk

1 cup flaked coconut
½ cup chopped nuts
1 cup almond brickle chips
   (optional)

▶ Combine all ingredients in bowl; mix well.
▶ Spread on warm cake.
▶ Broil until brown and bubbly.

CONFECTIONERS' SUGAR FROSTING

½ cup (1 stick) butter or
   margarine, softened
1½ teaspoons vanilla extract
1 egg white

¼ cup milk
1 16-ounce package
   confectioners' sugar

▶ Combine butter and vanilla in mixer bowl. Beat until light and fluffy.
▶ Add egg white, milk and confectioners' sugar. Beat until mixture is smooth and creamy.
▶ Yields enough for two 9-inch cake layers.

VARIATIONS

Chocolate—Add ¼ cup baking cocoa and enough additional milk to make smooth and creamy. Proceed as directed above.

Chocolate Chip—Add ½ cup miniature chocolate chips to vanilla or chocolate frosting.

Cinnamon—Add ¾ teaspoon cinnamon. Proceed as directed above.

Eggnog—Substitute dairy eggnog for milk. Proceed as directed above.

Mocha—Add 2 tablespoons cocoa and 3 tablespoons coffee and omit 3 tablespoons milk. Proceed as directed above.

Strawberry—Substitute one 10-ounce package thawed frozen strawberries for vanilla, egg white and milk. Proceed as directed above.

CREAM CHEESE FROSTING

½ cup (1 stick) butter or
   margarine, softened
8 ounces cream cheese,
   softened

1 16-ounce package
   confectioners' sugar
1 tablespoon vanilla extract

▶ Cream butter and cream cheese in mixer bowl until light and fluffy.
▶ Add confectioners' sugar gradually, beating until smooth and creamy. Blend in vanilla; beat well.
▶ Yields enough for two 9-inch cake layers.

VARIATIONS

Coconut—Add 1 cup coconut. Proceed as directed above.

Cranberry—Add ½ cup cranberry sauce. Proceed as directed above.

Maple—Substitute 1 tablespoon maple extract for vanilla. Proceed as directed above.

Pineapple—Add ¼ cup of canned drained, crushed pineapple. Proceed as directed above.

CONFECTIONERS' SUGAR GLAZE

1 cup confectioners' sugar   2 tablespoons lemon juice

▶ Combine confectioners' sugar and lemon juice in bowl; mix well.
▶ Drizzle over warm cake.
▶ Yields enough for 10-inch bundt or tube cake.

VARIATIONS

Substitute cream for lemon juice and add ¼ teaspoon cinnamon and nutmeg. Substitute orange juice concentrate for lemon juice.

MAKING A GOOD THING BETTER

Start with a cake mix and most of the work is done. Add a few extras and you'll have a special cake in no time.

ANGEL FOOD CAKE

▶ Buy only a 2-step angel food cake mix such as Duncan Hines. Prepare egg white mixture, Packet I, using package directions. Beat at the highest speed of electric mixer until very stiff peaks form. Do not underbeat.
▶ Sprinkle ¼ of the flour packet over egg whites. Fold in gently with rubber spatula (see page 35). Fold in remaining flour in 3 additions.
▶ Spoon into ungreased 10-inch tube pan. Run knife through batter about 1 inch from edge of pan. Bake using package directions.
▶ Invert on funnel. Cool completely. Loosen cake from side of pan with metal spatula. Invert onto cake plate.
▶ Yields 16 servings.

APPLE SPICE CAKE

1 17-ounce package spice cake mix
3 eggs
3 tablespoons water
1 21-ounce can apple pie filling
1 cup chopped pecans
¼ cup (½ stick) butter or margarine
½ cup sugar
½ cup flour
½ teaspoon cinnamon

▶ Preheat oven to 350 degrees. Grease and flour 9x13-inch cake pan.
▶ Combine cake mix, eggs and water in mixer bowl. Beat at medium speed for 2 minutes. Chop apples in pie filling. Add pie filling and ½ cup pecans to batter; mix well. Pour into prepared cake pan.
▶ Mix butter, sugar, flour, cinnamon and remaining ½ cup pecans in small bowl until mixture is crumbly. Sprinkle over batter.
▶ Bake for 30 to 35 minutes or until cake tests done. Cool completely in pan.
▶ Yields 12 servings.

CHOCOLATE CHERRY CAKE

1 17-ounce package chocolate cake mix
2 eggs

1 21-ounce can cherry pie filling
1 teaspoon almond extract

► Preheat oven to 350 degrees. Grease 9x13-inch cake pan.
► Combine dry cake mix, eggs, pie filling and almond extract in mixer bowl; mix well. Pour into prepared cake pan.
► Bake for 30 to 35 minutes or until cake tests done. Cool in cake pan.
► Yields 12 servings.

CREAM OF COCONUT CAKE

1 17-ounce package white cake mix
3 eggs
¼ cup oil
1 4-ounce can flaked coconut

1 cup sour cream
1 14-ounce can cream of coconut
1 4-ounce can flaked coconut
8 ounces whipped topping

► Preheat oven to 350 degrees. Grease 9x13-inch cake pan.
► Combine cake mix, eggs, oil, 1 can coconut and sour cream in mixer bowl. Beat at low speed of electric mixer until blended. Beat at high speed for 2 minutes. Pour into prepared pan.
► Bake for 20 minutes or until cake tests done. Pierce entire cake with fork.
► Pour cream of coconut over hot cake. Cool in pan.
► Mix remaining 1 can coconut and whipped topping in bowl. Spread over cooled cake. Cover with plastic wrap. Chill in refrigerator overnight.
► Yields 12 servings.

LUCIOUS LEMON CAKE

2 tablespoons lemon juice
1 17-ounce package lemon cake mix
1 4-ounce package lemon instant pudding mix

4 eggs
1 cup oil
1 cup water
2 cups confectioners' sugar
¼ cup lemon juice

► Preheat oven to 325 degrees. Grease bundt pan.
► Combine 2 tablespoons lemon juice, cake mix, pudding mix, eggs, oil and water in mixer bowl. Beat at medium speed for 2 minutes.
► Pour into prepared pan. Bake for 45 minutes or until cake tests done. Cool in pan for 10 minutes. Invert onto wire rack.
► Combine confectioners' sugar and lemon juice in small bowl; mix well. Pour glaze over cake.
► Yields 16 servings.

MYSTERY GERMAN CHOCOLATE CAKE

1 18-ounce package German chocolate cake mix	1 cup water
	⅓ cup milk
	¼ cup butter or margarine
1 cup sour cream	1 11-ounce package coconut-pecan frosting mix
3 eggs	

▶ Grease microwave-safe tube pan. Combine dry cake mix, sour cream, eggs and water in bowl; mix well. Pour into prepared pan.
▶ Mix milk and butter in glass bowl. Microwave on High (600 to 700 watts) for 1 minute. Stir in frosting mix. Spoon in circle on top of batter. Frosting should not touch side of pan. Cover with waxed paper. Place tube pan on inverted saucer in microwave.
▶ Microwave on Medium-High for 12 minutes or until cake tests almost done. Let stand for 10 minutes. Invert onto plate. Frosting will be on top.
▶ Yields 8 to 10 servings.

MOUND CAKE

2 cups sour cream	2 cups sugar
1 12-ounce package flaked coconut	1 17-ounce package devil's food cake mix

▶ Combine sour cream, coconut and sugar in mixer bowl; mix well. Chill in refrigerator overnight.
▶ Preheat oven to 350 degrees. Grease and flour two 9-inch round cake pans. Prepare cake mix according to package directions. Pour into pans.
▶ Bake for 20 minutes or until cake tests done. Cool in pans for 10 minutes. Invert onto cake racks to cool completely.
▶ Split each cake layer in half. Spread coconut mixture between layers and over top and side of cake. Chill for several hours.
▶ Yields 12 servings.

PINEAPPLE UPSIDE-DOWN CAKE

6 tablespoons melted margarine	7 slices canned pineapple
	7 maraschino cherries
1 cup packed light brown sugar	1 7-ounce package Jiffy yellow cake mix

▶ Preheat oven to 350 degrees.
▶ Cook margarine and brown sugar in saucepan over low heat until sugar dissolves, stirring constantly. Pour into 8-inch square cake pan.
▶ Arrange pineapple slices in pan. Place cherries in centers of slices.
▶ Prepare cake mix using package directions. Pour over pineapple.
▶ Bake for 30 minutes. Invert onto cake plate immediately. Cut into squares.
▶ Yields 6 servings.

STRAWBERRY SHORTCUT CAKE

Strawberries sink to the bottom and marshmallows rise to the top.

1   3-ounce package strawberry gelatin
3   10-ounce packages frozen sweetened strawberries, thawed
3   eggs

1   15-ounce package white cake mix
1   cup oil
¾   cup water
2   cups miniature marshmallows

▶ Preheat oven to 350 degrees. Grease 9x13-inch cake pan.
▶ Mix dry gelatin and strawberries in bowl. Combine eggs, cake mix, oil and water in mixer bowl. Beat at high speed for 2 minutes.
▶ Sprinkle marshmallows in bottom of cake pan. Pour batter on top. Spoon strawberry mixture over batter.
▶ Bake for 40 minutes or until cake tests done. Cool in pan. Cut into squares. Turn each serving upside down on dessert plate.
▶ Yields 8 servings.

CRAZY CAKE

2 cups sugar
3 cups flour
½ cup cocoa
2 teaspoons soda

1 tablespoon vanilla extract
2 tablespoons vinegar
¾ cup oil
2 cups water

▶ Preheat oven to 350 degrees. Grease 9x13-inch cake pan.
▶ Combine sugar, flour, cocoa and soda in sifter. Sift into prepared pan.
▶ Make 3 wells in dry ingredients. Pour vanilla into 1 well, vinegar into 1 well and oil into remaining well. Pour water over all. Mix with fork until smooth.
▶ Bake for 30 minutes or until cake tests done. Cool in pan. Frost cool cake as desired.
▶ Yields 12 servings.

SOUR CREAM POUND CAKE

1 cup (2 sticks) butter
3 cups sugar
6 eggs
8 ounces sour cream

3 cups flour
¼ teaspoon soda
⅛ teaspoon salt
1 teaspoon vanilla extract

▶ Preheat oven to 325 degrees. Grease and flour 10-inch tube pan.
▶ Cream butter and sugar in mixer bowl at high speed until light and fluffy.
▶ Blend in eggs 1 at a time. Blend in sour cream.
▶ Add mixture of flour, soda and salt to batter; mix well. Blend in vanilla.
▶ Pour into cake pan. Bake for 1 hour and 10 minutes or until cake tests done. Cool in pan for 10 minutes. Invert onto wire rack to cool completely.
▶ Yields 12 to 16 servings.

The Cookie Monster

◆ ◆ ◆ ◆ ◆ ◆ ◆ ◆ ◆ ◆ ◆

Cookies

◆ ◆ ◆ ◆ ◆ ◆ ◆

If your idea of cookies goes no further than chocolate chip, this chapter may enlarge your horizons. Cookies come in all shapes, sizes and flavors. Cookies can be crisp, chewy or tender enough to melt in your mouth. Cookies can be so teeny that they can be eaten by the handful like peanuts or so large that careful cutting will satisfy a bunch. Cookies can be sinfully rich and full of calories or deliciously nutritious.

Cookies can be quick and easy or frighteningly time consuming and difficult. Fortunately for you, the selection here ranges from very easy to relatively easy. Once mastered, each recipe can be varied so your friends will think of you as a talented cookie-maker.

COOKIE BAKING TIPS

► Most cookies are baked on greased cookie sheets but when an ungreased cookie sheet is called for, be sure to use it.
► Arrange cookies on the cookie sheet so they have plenty of room to spread without running together. Thin cookie dough will spread more than stiffer dough.
► Bake cookies on the rack in the center of the oven with the cookie sheet or pan in the center of the rack to allow space for the heat to circulate.
► Set timer for minimum baking time. If cookies need more time to bake, watch carefully to avoid overbrowning.
► Store crisp cookies and chewy cookies in separate containers or they will all turn out tough and soggy.

EASY PEANUT BUTTER KISS COOKIES

1 roll refrigerator peanut
  butter cookie dough
	1 14-ounce package milk
	  chocolate kisses

- ▶ Preheat oven, slice and arrange cookies on cookie sheet following the directions on the cookie dough package. Do not flatten with fork.
- ▶ Bake the cookies according to package directions for 1 to 2 minutes less than directions indicate or until cookies are puffy and just starting to brown around edges.
- ▶ Remove cookie sheet from oven. Press chocolate kiss into the center of each cookie (unwrapped of course) so that outer edge of cookie stands up around base of kiss.
- ▶ Return to oven for 1 to 2 minutes if a crispy cookie is desired or remove cookies to wire rack to cool if chewier cookie is desired.
- ▶ Yields 2½ to 3 dozen.

VARIATION

Substitute chocolate stars, giant chocolate chips, jelly beans or miniature chocolate-covered peanut butter cups for the kisses. Combine and bake as directed above.

COOKIES FROM A CAKE MIX

1 17-ounce package any flavor cake mix	½ cup oil 2 eggs

- ▶ Preheat oven to 325 degrees.
- ▶ Combine dry cake mix, oil and eggs in bowl; mix well.
- ▶ Drop by teaspoonfuls onto greased cookie sheet.
- ▶ Bake for 10 minutes. Cool on cookie sheet for 1 minute.
- ▶ Remove to wire rack to cool completely.
- ▶ Yields 4 to 5 dozen.

VARIATIONS

Double Chocolate—Use a chocolate cake mix and add 1 to 2 cups chocolate chips. Combine and bake as directed above.

Chocolate Chip—Use a yellow cake mix and add 2 cups chocolate chips. Combine and bake as directed above.

Coconut Almond—Use a white cake mix and add 1 cup shredded coconut and 1 teaspoon almond extract. Combine and bake as directed above.

Banana Spice—Use a spice cake mix and add ½ cup mashed banana and ½ cup chopped pecans. Combine and bake as directed above.

Lemon Oatmeal—Use a lemon cake mix, only 1 egg and add ¼ cup packed brown sugar and ¾ cup oats. Combine and bake as directed above.

LEMON WHIPPER SNAPPERS

1 17-ounce package lemon
   cake mix
2 cups whipped topping

1 egg
Confectioners' sugar

► Preheat oven to 350 degrees.
► Combine dry cake mix, whipped topping and egg in bowl; mix well. Chill in refrigerator for 15 minutes for easier handling.
► Spread about 1 cup confectioners' sugar in small shallow bowl such as a cereal or soup bowl. Drop cookie dough 1 teaspoonful at a time into confectioners' sugar; roll dough gently with fingertip or spoon until coated. Place dough 2 inches apart on lightly greased cookie sheet.
► Bake for 10 minutes or until golden. Cool on cookie sheet for 1 minute. Remove to wire rack to cool completely.
► Yields 4 dozen.

COCONUT AND CREAM CHEESE DROPS

¼ cup (½ stick) butter or
   margarine, softened
8 ounces cream cheese,
   softened
1 egg

¼ teaspoon almond extract
1 17-ounce package white
   cake mix
1 cup flaked coconut

► Preheat oven to 375 degrees.
► Beat butter and cream cheese in mixer bowl at medium speed until light and fluffy.
► Add egg, almond extract and about half the dry cake mix; beat until smooth. Add remaining cake mix and coconut; mix well with spoon.
► Drop by teaspoonfuls about 2 inches apart onto ungreased cookie sheet. Bake for 8 to 10 minutes or until very light golden brown. Cool on cookie sheet for 1 to 2 minutes. Remove to wire rack to cool completely.
► Yields 5 dozen.

UNBELIEVABLY EASY PEANUT BUTTER COOKIES

1 cup peanut butter
1 cup sugar

1 egg
1 teaspoon vanilla extract

► Preheat oven to 350 degrees.
► Combine peanut butter, sugar, egg and vanilla in bowl; mix well with wooden spoon. Shape by tablespoonfuls into balls; place about 2 inches apart on lightly greased cookie sheet.
► Flatten to ¼-inch thickness by pressing in crisscross design with fork.
► Bake for 10 minutes or until golden brown. Cool on cookie sheet for 1 minute. Remove to wire rack to cool completely.
► Yields 1 to 1½ dozen.

BAR COOKIE MAGIC

You can cut bar cookies several ways in order to yield the number of cookies needed.

Pan Size	Number of cuts Lengthwise	Crosswise	Yield
8x8-inch	3	3	1⅓ dozen
	3	5	2 dozen
9x13-inch	2	7	2 dozen
	5	5	3 dozen
	7	5	4 dozen
10x15-inch	3	8	3 dozen
	3	11	4 dozen
	3	14	5 dozen
	7	8	6 dozen

DESIGNER BROWNIES

1   15-ounce package fudge brownie mix
½ cup chopped pecans (optional)
¼ cup chopped drained maraschino cherries (optional)
3 tablespoons chunky peanut butter (optional)
1 cup miniature marshmallows (optional)
1 cup semisweet chocolate chips (optional)

▶ Mix the brownie mix following the directions on the package. Add 1 or more of the optional ingredients; mix well.
▶ Bake according to the package directions. Cool. Cut into squares or bars.
▶ Yields 3 dozen.

VARIATIONS

Orange—Substitute ¼ cup orange juice for ¼ cup of the water. Bake as directed above.

Double Chocolate—Arrange milk chocolate candy bars, chocolate chips or chocolate-covered peppermint patties over the hot baked layer. Return to the oven for 1 minute or until softened. Spread or swirl with knife to cover completely. Cool and cut as desired.

SAUCEPAN BROWNIES

½ cup (1 stick) butter
2 ounces unsweetened
  baking chocolate
1 cup sugar

2 eggs
½ cup flour
1 teaspoon vanilla extract
1 cup chopped pecans

▶ Preheat oven to 350 degrees.
▶ Combine butter and chocolate in medium saucepan over low heat. Heat until butter and chocolate melt, stirring constantly. Remove from heat.
▶ Add sugar and eggs; mix well. Add flour and vanilla; mix well. Stir in pecans. Pour into greased 9x9-inch baking pan.
▶ Bake in preheated oven for 30 minutes or until brownies pull slightly from side of pan. Cool on wire rack. Cut into squares.
▶ Yields 2 dozen.

BAKED GRANOLA BARS

1¼ cups packed brown sugar
¾ cup (1½ sticks) butter
4 cups oats

¾ cup raisins
1 cup chopped pecans
1 tablespoon cinnamon

▶ Preheat oven to 350 degrees.
▶ Place brown sugar and butter in 9x13-inch baking pan. Heat in oven until butter melts, stirring occasionally. Remove from oven.
▶ Add oats, raisins, pecans and cinnamon; mix with wooden spoon or pancake turner. Press mixture firmly into pan.
▶ Bake for 30 minutes or until light brown. Cool in pan on wire rack for 15 minutes. Cut into bars. Cool completely. Store in airtight container.
▶ Yields 3 dozen.

SEVEN-LAYER COOKIE BARS

2 cups graham cracker
  crumbs
½ cup (1 stick) melted butter
3 cups semisweet chocolate
  chips

3 cups butterscotch chips
1   14-ounce can sweetened
  condensed milk
2 cups flaked coconut
1 cup chopped pecans

▶ Preheat oven to 350 degrees.
▶ Mix graham cracker crumbs and melted butter in bowl with fork. Press over bottom of 10x15-inch baking pan to form crust.
▶ Sprinkle chocolate chips and butterscotch chips over crust. Drizzle sweetened condensed milk over chips. Sprinkle coconut and pecans over top.
▶ Bake for 15 to 20 minutes or until light brown. Cool. Cut into bars.
▶ Yields 5 dozen.

WORLD'S BEST AND EASIEST OATMEAL COOKIE

1¼ cups oats
1 cup flour
½ cup sugar
½ cup packed light brown
  sugar
½ teaspoon salt
½ teaspoon soda

1 cup flaked or shredded
  coconut (optional)
½ cup raisins
½ cup oil
1 egg
1 teaspoon vanilla extract

▶ Preheat oven to 325 degrees.
▶ Combine oats, flour, sugar, brown sugar, salt, soda, coconut and raisins in large bowl; mix well.
▶ Add oil, egg and vanilla; mix well. Mixture will seem dry and crumbly.
▶ Shape by tablespoonfuls into balls, pressing to make mixture cling together. Place 2 inches apart on ungreased cookie sheet.
▶ Bake for 12 to 15 minutes or until light brown. Cookies will be chewy if baked until just starting to brown and will be crispier if baked for slightly longer. Cool on wire rack.
▶ Yields 2½ to 3 dozen.

CHEWY CHOCOLATE CHIP BARS

2 cups packed brown sugar
¾ cup oil
3 eggs
2 teaspoons vanilla extract
2 cups all-purpose flour

1 teaspoon baking powder
¼ teaspoon soda
¼ teaspoon salt
2 cups chocolate chips
1 cup chopped pecans

▶ Preheat oven to 375 degrees.
▶ Combine brown sugar, oil, eggs and vanilla in bowl; mix until smooth. Add flour, baking powder, soda and salt; mix well.
▶ Add chocolate chips and pecans; mix well. Pour into greased 9x13-inch baking pan.
▶ Bake for 10 minutes. Remove from oven. Shake pan and rap sharply on counter (right side up). Reduce oven temperature to 350 degrees. Bake for 15 minutes longer or until brown. Cool on wire rack. Cut into bars.
▶ Yields 3 dozen.

VARIATION

Add ½ cup flaked coconut, raisins or chopped dates. Bake as directed above.

CHOCOLATE CHIP DROP COOKIES

⅔ cup shortening
⅔ cup butter, softened
1 cup sugar
1 cup packed light brown
   sugar
2 eggs
2 teaspoons vanilla extract

3 cups flour
1 teaspoon soda
1 teaspoon salt
1 cup chopped pecans
2 cups semisweet chocolate
   chips

▶ Preheat oven to 375 degrees.
▶ Combine shortening, butter, sugar and brown sugar in mixer bowl. Beat at low speed until light and fluffy. Add eggs and vanilla; beat until smooth and creamy.
▶ Mix flour, soda and salt in small bowl. Add flour mixture about a cup at a time to butter and sugar mixture, stirring with a wooden spoon until well mixed after each addition. Stir in pecans and chocolate chips.
▶ Drop cookie dough by rounded teaspoonfuls about 2 inches apart onto greased cookie sheet.
▶ Bake for 8 minutes or until light brown. Cool on cookie sheet for 2 minutes. Remove to wire rack to cool completely. Store in airtight container.
▶ Yields 7 dozen.

VARIATIONS

Chocolate Chip Bars—Grease two 9x13-inch baking pans lightly. Divide cookie dough between the 2 pans and spread dough evenly in pans with back of spoon. Bake at 350 degrees for about 30 minutes or until golden brown and the cookies pull slightly from the side of the pan. Cool on wire rack. Cut into squares or bars.

Giant Chocolate Chip—Divide cookie dough among 4 or 5 lightly greased pie plates and spread evenly. Bake at 350 degrees for 20 minutes or until golden brown. Cut into wedges when cool. These make wonderful gifts.

Different Chip—Substitute mint chocolate, milk chocolate, white chocolate, butterscotch or almond brickle chips for semisweet chocolate chips. Bake as directed above.

Fruity Chip—Add ½ cup chopped dates, ½ cup raisins or ½ cup coconut. Bake as directed above.

Nutty Chip—Substitute walnuts or macadamia nuts for pecans. Bake as directed above.

The
Pie's
The Limit

◆ ◆ ◆ ◆ ◆ ◆ ◆ ◆ ◆ ◆ ◆

◆ ◆ ◆ ◆ ◆ **Pies** ◆ ◆ ◆ ◆ ◆

Any dish covered on top or cushioned underneath with a crust is a pie, a dish which has been popular for over 500 years. Although Little Jack Horner's Christmas pie was probably a meat delicacy, an American pie is almost always a dessert. Today, the crust can vary from cookie or cracker crumbs to homemade pastry while the covering might be whipped topping, meringue, or nothing at all. The fillings can be puddings, fruit, ice cream, anything. The combinations are infinite. Our recipes begin with the easiest possible and progress to more challenging recipes as your skill improves. Improvise your own combination—you can't go wrong.

EASY AS PIE

Start with a ready-made graham cracker or chocolate cookie crumb crust. Fill it with one of these easy fillings for a no-cook pie.

Ice cream—Use 1 to 3 of your favorite flavors and top with ice cream topping and nuts.

Frozen yogurt—Top with fruit.

Flavored yogurt—Mix with fruit to match the flavor.

Whipped topping—Mix with fruit pie filling, crushed Oreos, crushed candy bars, or chocolate chips and miniature marshmallows.

Whipped cream cheese—Top with fruit pie filling or fresh fruit.

Marshmallow creme—Mix marshmallow creme and fresh fruit.

EVERYBODY'S FAVORITE PUDDING PIE

1　6-ounce package instant
　　pudding mix
2¾ cups milk
1　9-inch graham cracker
　　pie shell

1　8-ounce container
　　whipped topping
½ cup finely chopped pecans

▶ Combine dry pudding mix and milk in bowl; mix according to package directions. Pour into pie shell. Place plastic wrap over top of filling to seal and prevent rubbery top.
▶ Refrigerate until serving time; remove plastic wrap. Spread with whipped topping. Sprinkle with pecans.
▶ Yields 6 to 8 servings.

VARIATIONS

Coconut—Use coconut pudding, mixed with ½ cup shredded coconut and garnish with ½ cup shredded coconut. Combine as directed above.

Banana—Use banana pudding, mixed with ½ cup chopped banana and garnish with banana slices just before serving. Combine as directed above.

Rocky Road—Use chocolate pudding, mixed with ½ cup miniature chocolate chips and ½ cup miniature marshmallows and garnish top of pie with chocolate chips. Combine as directed above.

LEMONADE PIE

This pie always gets rave reviews—only you know how quick it is.

1　6-ounce can frozen
　　lemonade concentrate
1　14-ounce can sweetened
　　condensed milk

1　12-ounce container
　　whipped topping
1　9-inch graham cracker
　　pie shell

▶ Thaw lemonade concentrate. Combine lemonade concentrate and condensed milk in bowl; stir until smooth and well blended. Fold in about ⅔ of the whipped topping. Pour into pie shell; smooth top.
▶ Refrigerate until serving time. Garnish with lemon twists and dollops of remaining whipped topping.
▶ Yields 6 to 8 servings.

VARIATIONS

Pink Lemonade—Use pink lemonade and garnish with lemon twists and maraschino cherries. Combine as directed above.

Lime—Use limeade and garnish with lime twists. Combine as directed above.

Orange—Use orange juice and garnish with orange twists. Combine as directed above.

FROZEN PEANUT BUTTER PIE

Make this pie ahead to store in the freezer and you always have dessert on hand.

1 quart vanilla ice cream
1   8-ounce container
   whipped topping
½ cup chunky peanut butter

1   9-inch graham cracker or
   chocolate crumb pie shell
½ cup chocolate syrup

▶ Let ice cream stand at room temperature just until softened. Place in bowl. Add whipped topping and peanut butter; mix well.
▶ Spoon ice cream mixture into pie shell; smooth top. Cover with plastic wrap. Freeze for several hours or until firm. Store in freezer.
▶ Let stand at room temperature for 10 minutes or in refrigerator for 30 to 45 minutes or until slightly softened. Drizzle chocolate syrup over top just before serving. Store any remaining pie in freezer.
▶ Yields 6 to 8 servings.

VARIATIONS

Strawberry—Use strawberry ice cream topping and garnish with sliced fresh strawberries and whipped topping. Combine as directed above.

Caramel—Use caramel ice cream topping and garnish with coarsely crushed toffee or chopped pecans. Combine as directed above.

CRUMB PIE SHELL

Making your own crumb pie shell is simple and you can use whatever you like best. Baking is optional.

¼ cup butter or margarine
2 tablespoons sugar

1¼ cups fine vanilla wafer
   crumbs

▶ Preheat oven to 350 degrees.
▶ Melt butter in small saucepan over low heat; remove from heat.
▶ Mix sugar and crumbs in small bowl. Add melted butter; mix well with fork. Press evenly with back of spoon or fingertips over bottom and side of 9-inch pie plate.
▶ Bake in preheated oven for 10 minutes. Place on wire rack to cool.
▶ Yields 1 pie shell.

VARIATION

Use chocolate cookie crumbs, graham cracker crumbs, lemon wafer crumbs or gingersnap crumbs for a variety of pie shell flavors.

CHEESECAKE PIE

This pie can make your reputation as a cook but your blender does most of the work.

8 ounces cream cheese,
  softened
⅔ cup sugar
½ teaspoon almond extract
⅛ teaspoon salt
3 eggs

1 baked 9-inch Crumb Pie
  Shell (page 140)
1 20-ounce can cherry pie
  filling
1 cup whipping cream,
  whipped

► Preheat oven to 350 degrees.
► Combine cream cheese, sugar, almond flavoring, salt and eggs in mixer bowl or blender container.
► Beat or process until smooth and well blended. Stop the mixer or blender frequently to scrape the bowl or container with a rubber spatula.
► Pour into Crumb Pie Shell; smooth top.
► Bake in preheated oven for 30 minutes. Cool on wire rack.
► Spoon pie filling over cream cheese layer. Cover with plastic wrap. Refrigerate until serving time. Top with whipped cream.
► Yields 8 servings.

VARIATION

Use any other pie filling flavors and try different flavored pie shells.

EASY TWO-CRUST FRUIT PIE

2 frozen pie shells, thawed
1 20-ounce can pie filling

2 to 3 tablespoons milk
1 tablespoon sugar

► Preheat oven to 425.
► Use 1 pie shell in foil pie plate. If any breaks or tears are visible in dough, press with moistened fingertips to seal.
► Pour pie filling into pie shell. Moisten edge of pie shell with milk. Remove second pie shell from pie plate; place over top of pie. Press top and bottom shells together to seal. Fold edges under and flute following the directions on page 142.
► Cut several 1-inch slits in top crust to allow steam to escape while baking and prevent a soggy crust. Brush top crust lightly with milk and sprinkle with sugar.
► Bake for 40 minutes or until crust is golden brown. Cool on wire rack for 30 minutes or longer before cutting.
► Yields 6 to 8 servings.

VARIATION

Use prepared blueberry, apple or cherry pie filling or one of our homemade fillings on page 142. Bake as directed above.

HOMEMADE CHERRY PIE FILLING

1 16-ounce can water-pack
   sour cherries
¾ cup sugar
⅛ teaspoon salt

2½ tablespoons minute
   tapioca
¼ teaspoon almond extract

▶ Mix all ingredients in bowl. Let stand for 15 minutes. Pour into pie shell. Bake as instructed on page 141.

HOMEMADE APPLE PIE FILLING

6 cups sliced peeled tart
   apples
½ cup sugar

½ teaspoon cinnamon
2 tablespoons butter

▶ Toss apples with mixture of sugar and cinnamon. Pour into pie shell. Dot with butter before adding top crust. Bake as instructed on page 141.

BAKING A PIE SHELL

▶ Preheat oven as directed on package.
▶ Remove wrappings from frozen pie shell in foil pie plate or fit 1 of the refrigerator pie pastries into your own pie plate, pressing gently from center to edge to remove air bubbles.
▶ Fold edge of pastry under to make stand-up edge on top of pie plate rim. Place 1 index finger on inside edge and pinch pastry at ¼-inch intervals with index finger and thumb of other hand to make fluted edge.
▶ Prick shell with a fork in many places over bottom and side. This is necessary to prevent the shell from puffing and blistering.
▶ Bake in preheated oven for time specified in directions but watch closely starting a minute or 2 before minimum time specified in case shell browns quickly. Do not overbrown. Place baked pie shell on wire rack to cool.

FRESH STRAWBERRY PIE

3 cups fresh strawberries
1 baked 9-inch pie shell
1 cup sugar
3 tablespoons cornstarch
2 tablespoons light corn syrup

Pinch of salt
2 teaspoons strawberry
   gelatin
Red food coloring

▶ Arrange strawberries in pie shell. Cook sugar, cornstarch, corn syrup and salt in saucepan over low heat until thick and clear, stirring constantly.
▶ Add gelatin and food coloring. Stir until gelatin is dissolved. Cool slightly.
▶ Pour glaze over strawberries. Chill until serving time. Garnish with whipped cream and additional strawberries.
▶ Yields 6 servings.

CHOCOLATE MERINGUE PIE

Perfect meringue is the mark of a good pie and anyone can do it.

1 6-ounce package pudding and pie filling mix (not instant)
2¾ cups milk

1 9-inch baked pie shell
4 egg whites
½ cup sugar

► Preheat oven to 350 degrees. Read pages 34 and 35.
► Place dry pudding mix in saucepan. Add milk gradually, mixing well. Cook over medium heat until mixture comes to a boil, stirring constantly. Pour into pie shell.
► Beat egg whites in mixer bowl until soft peaks form. Add sugar 1 table-spoon at a time, beating constantly until stiff peaks form.
► Spread over pudding with knife, sealing meringue to pie shell at edge of pudding. Touch meringue lightly with knife and lift small peaks of me-ringue over entire surface.
► Bake for 15 minutes or until meringue peaks are golden brown. Let pie stand until cool. Store in refrigerator.
► Yields 6 to 8 servings.

VARIATIONS

Coconut Cream—Use coconut pudding and sprinkle coconut over me-ringue before baking as directed above.

Banana Cream—Use vanilla pudding mixed with sliced bananas. Combine and bake as directed above.

Black Bottom—Use hot vanilla pudding spread over ½ cup semisweet chocolate chips sprinkled in pie shell. Combine and bake as directed above.

Butterscotch Toffee—Use butterscotch pudding sprinkled with crushed Heath bars. Combine and bake as directed above.

Lemon—Use lemon pudding mixed with 1 teaspoon grated lemon rind. Combine and bake as directed above.

Pineapple Cream—Make vanilla pudding using 1¼ cups pineapple juice, 1¼ cups milk. Stir in ½ cup crushed pineapple. Combine and bake as directed above.

Chocolate-Mint—Use chocolate pudding mixed with 1 teaspoon pepper-mint extract. Combine and bake as directed above.

Chocolate-Mocha—Use chocolate pudding made with 1 teaspoon instant coffee powder dissolved in the milk. Combine and bake as directed above.

Piña Colada—Use coconut cream pudding mixed with ½ cup drained crushed pineapple after cooking. Combine and bake as directed above.

MAKE-YOUR-OWN PIE PASTRY

2 cups flour
1 teaspoon salt

⅔ cup shortening
¼ cup (about) cold water

▶ Mix flour and salt in bowl. Add shortening; cut into flour with pastry blender or 2 knives used scissor-fashion until mixture appears crumbly with particles the size of small peas or smaller.

▶ Add water 1 tablespoon at a time, tossing mixture lightly with fork until dough clings together. Shape into ball; wrap in plastic wrap. Let stand at room temperature for 5 minutes. Shape dough into 2 balls which can be used for 2 pie shells or for the crusts of a 2-crust pie.

ROLLING THE PASTRY

▶ Sprinkle a clean dry surface with about ¼ cup flour; roll a rolling pin through the flour to coat the rolling pin and spread the flour.
▶ Flatten 1 of the dough balls slightly; place in center of floured area.
▶ Place the rolling pin in the center of the ball; roll from center to edge in all directions to make a circle 2 inches larger than the pie plate. Lift the dough occasionally to make sure it is not sticking; if it does stick, lift carefully and sprinkle a small amount of additional flour on the work surface.
▶ Mend any tears or cracks by moistening the torn edges with water and patching with a small amount of dough cut from the outer edge of the circle. Do not wad up into ball and reroll because the crust will be tough.
▶ Place rolling pin at edge of dough circle. Roll dough loosely onto rolling pin; lift onto pie plate. Place rolling pin at edge of pie plate allowing about a 1-inch overhang. Unroll dough gently over pie plate; set rolling pin aside. Press dough gently over bottom and side of pie plate; do not stretch dough or allow air bubbles to occur between dough and pie plate.

BAKING THE PIE SHELL

▶ Preheat oven to 425 degrees.
▶ Press edge with fork or pinch into high edge, flute and trim excess.
▶ When a recipe specifies an unbaked pie shell, add the filling and bake according to recipe instructions. When a recipe specifies a baked pie shell, prick bottom and side of shell in many places with fork to prevent puffing.
▶ Bake in oven for 15 minutes or until golden. Cool completely.
▶ Yields 2 pie shells or pastry for one 2-crust pie.

Sweet Nothings

Desserts

Desserts can be as simple—and as good—as fresh fruit or your favorite yogurt. For those times when you want something more elaborate—but not much more difficult—our recipes will make a super ending to any menu.

ICE CREAM DESSERTS

PERFECT SUNDAES AND PARFAITS

The difference between sundaes and parfaits is just the appearance. The toppings and crunchies which are spooned over the ice cream in a sundae are layered between spoonfuls in a parfait. Served in tall glasses, the parfait makes an elegant dessert out of a childhood favorite. Use one or more choices from each column for your own creations!

Basics	Toppings	Sprinkles
Frozen yogurt	Ice cream syrups	Cookie crumbs
Ice cream	Crushed pineapple	Nuts
Ice milk	Fresh fruit	Granola
Sherbet	Pie filling	Raisins
Sorbet	Jam or preserves	M and M's
Pudding	Marshmallow creme	Crushed candy
Yogurt	Frozen fruit,	Trail mix
Jell-O cubes	slightly thawed	Chocolate chips

BAKED ALASKA

A base of cake, a scoop of ice cream, a fluffy covering of meringue make a fascinating fire and ice combination. The secret is to freeze the cake and ice cream, to seal meringue to surface of the baking sheet and to bake in a very hot oven for just a few minutes. Make yours on a cake layer or in individual servings.

Sponge cake dessert cups   Meringue (See page 143)
Ice cream

▶ Preheat oven to 450 degrees.
▶ Place sponge cake cups on foil-covered baking sheet.
▶ Top with scoops of ice cream. Freeze until firm.
▶ Cover thickly with meringue, sealing to foil.
▶ Bake for 1 to 2 minutes or until meringue is golden. Serve immediately.

VARIATIONS

Ice Cream Sandwich Alaskas—Use ice cream sandwich halves for base and ice cream; cover with meringue and bake as above.

Mint Patty Alaskas—Use frozen ice cream mint patties for ice cream; cover with meringue, and bake as above.

Volcano—Pack ½ gallon ice cream into 2-quart bowl. Freeze until firm. Unmold ice cream onto cake layer. Cover with meringue. Bake as above. Place lighted candle in top.

Substitute large cookies, cupcakes, pound cake slices, brownies or jelly roll slices for sponge cake dessert cups.

TURTLE ICE CREAM DESSERT

20 Oreo cookies, crushed
¼ cup melted butter and
   margarine
1 pint caramel ice cream,
   softened
¾ cup chopped pecans

1 8-ounce jar caramel ice
cream topping
1 8-ounce container
whipped topping
1 1-serving envelope cocoa
mix

▶ Combine cookies and butter in bowl; mix well. Press into 9-inch square baking dish.
▶ Mix ice cream and ¾ cup pecans in bowl. Spoon over cookies.
▶ Drizzle caramel topping over ice cream. Spread half the whipped topping over ice cream.
▶ Blend remaining whipped topping and cocoa mix in bowl. Spread over top of ice cream.
▶ Freeze for several hours. Cut into squares.
▶ Yields 9 servings.

PUDDING DESSERTS

Start with pudding mix and create to your heart's content.

CHOCOLATE ECLAIR DESSERT

3 cups milk
2   4-ounce packages vanilla
   instant pudding mix
1   16-ounce package
   graham crackers
2 tablespoons baking cocoa

6 tablespoons (¾ stick)
   melted butter
1 teaspoon vanilla extract
¼ cup milk or coffee
1½ cups confectioners' sugar

▶ Combine milk and pudding mix in bowl according to package directions.
▶ Arrange layer of graham crackers in 9x13-inch dish. Cover with pudding. Repeat layers with remaining graham crackers and pudding, ending with graham crackers.
▶ Combine cocoa, butter, vanilla, milk and confectioners' sugar in bowl; mix well. Spread over graham crackers.
▶ Chill for 24 hours.
▶ Yields 12 to 16 servings.

MISSISSIPPI MUD

1 cup confectioners' sugar
8 ounces cream cheese,
   softened
1   16-ounce container
   whipped topping

Crunchy Pecan Crust
1   6-ounce package chocolate
   instant pudding mix
3 cups milk

▶ Combine confectioners' sugar, cream cheese and half the whipped topping in mixer bowl. Beat until smooth.
▶ Spread cream cheese mixture over cooled Crunchy Pecan Crust.
▶ Prepare pudding mix with milk according to package directions. Spread over cream cheese layer.
▶ Spread remaining whipped topping over top. Chill until serving time.
▶ Yields 12 servings.

CRUNCHY PECAN CRUST

1 cup flour
1 cup chopped pecans

½ cup melted butter or
   margarine

▶ Preheat oven to 350 degrees.
▶ Combine flour, pecans and butter in bowl; mix well. Press into bottom of 9-inch square baking dish.
▶ Bake for 15 minutes. Let stand until cool.

VARIATIONS

Butterscotch—Use 6-ounce package butterscotch pudding mix. Combine as directed on page 148.

Lemon Lush—Use 6-ounce package lemon pudding mix. Combine as directed on page 148.

Pistachio Delight—Use 6-ounce package pistachio pudding mix. Combine as directed on page 148.

RICH BANANA PUDDING

1 4-ounce package vanilla instant pudding mix
1¾ cups milk
1 cup sour cream
1 8-ounce container whipped topping
72 vanilla wafers
3 large bananas, sliced

▶ Combine pudding mix and milk in bowl; beat until thickened.
▶ Fold in sour cream and whipped topping.
▶ Layer vanilla wafers, banana slices and pudding mixture ⅓ at a time in serving dish.
▶ Chill in refrigerator until serving time.
▶ Yields 6 servings.

FRUIT DESSERTS

Fruit, fresh or dressed up in the following ways, is a delicious dessert.

APPLE CRISP

5 cups sliced tart apples
¼ cup orange juice
¾ cup flour
½ cup oats
1 cup sugar
1 teaspoon cinnamon
¼ teaspoon nutmeg
½ cup (1 stick) butter

▶ Preheat oven to 375 degrees.
▶ Arrange apple slices in 8x8-inch baking dish. Apples may be peeled or unpeeled. Core should be removed before slicing. Add orange juice.
▶ Combine flour, oats, sugar, cinnamon and nutmeg in bowl; mix well. Cut in butter with pastry cutter until crumbly.
▶ Sprinkle crumbs over apples. Bake for 45 minutes or until apples are tender. Serve warm with ice cream or whipped topping.
▶ Yields 6 servings.

VARIATION

Substitute berries, cherries, peaches or rhubarb for apples. Season with sugar to taste before topping with crumbs.

BANANA SPLIT DESSERT

½ cup melted butter
3 cups graham cracker
  crumbs
2 eggs
1 cup butter, softened
2 cups confectioners' sugar
1 20-ounce can crushed
  pineapple, drained

5 large bananas, sliced
1 16-ounce container frozen
  whipped topping
¼ cup chocolate sauce
¼ cup chopped nuts
¼ cup chopped maraschino
  cherries

► Combine melted butter and graham cracker crumbs in bowl; mix well. Pat into 9x13-inch dish.
► Mix eggs, softened butter and confectioners' sugar in mixer bowl. Beat at high speed with electric mixer for 5 minutes. Spread over crust.
► Layer pineapple and bananas over filling. Spread whipped topping over fruit. Drizzle chocolate sauce over top. Sprinkle with nuts and cherries.
► Chill in refrigerator for 4 hours to overnight.
► Yields 12 servings.

QUICK COBBLER

½ cup (1 stick) margarine
1 cup milk
1 cup self-rising flour

1 cup sugar
1 cup sliced apples,
  peaches or berries

► Preheat oven to 375 degrees.
► Place margarine in 9x13-inch baking dish. Heat in oven until melted.
► Combine milk, self-rising flour and sugar in bowl. Pour into melted margarine; do not stir. Arrange fruit on top; do not stir.
► Bake for 40 minutes or until light brown. Serve warm with ice cream.
► Yields 9 servings.

FRUIT AND CREAM DESSERT PIZZA

1 18-ounce package
  refrigerator cookie dough
8 ounces cream cheese,
  softened

⅓ cup sugar
1 teaspoon vanilla extract
2 cups sliced strawberries or
  mixture of fruit

► Preheat oven to 375 degrees.
► Slice cookie dough into ⅛-inch slices. Arrange on 14-inch pizza pan in circular pattern, overlapping slices slightly.
► Bake for 12 minutes. Cool completely.
► Combine cream cheese, sugar and vanilla in mixer bowl. Beat until light and fluffy. Spread on cookie crust.
► Arrange fruit over filling. Chill until serving time. Cut into wedges.
► Yields 10 servings.

FROSTY STRAWBERRY SQUARES

Crunchy Pecan Crust
(page 148)
1   10-ounce package frozen
strawberries, partially
thawed

⅔ cup sugar
2 egg whites
2 tablespoons lemon juice
1   8-ounce container whipped
topping

▶ Prepare and bake Crunchy Pecan Crust in 9x13-inch baking dish. Stir until crumbly. Cool. Remove ⅓ of the crumbs; spread remaining crumbs.
▶ Combine strawberries, sugar, egg whites and lemon juice in mixer bowl.
▶ Beat at highest speed of electric mixer for 20 minutes or until very stiff peaks form. Do not underbeat.
▶ Fold in whipped topping gently. Spoon into prepared dish. Sprinkle with remaining crumbs. Freeze until firm. Cut into squares.
▶ Yields 12 servings.

EASY CREAM PUFFS

1 cup water
½ cup (1 stick) butter

1 cup flour
4 eggs

▶ Preheat oven to 375 degrees.
▶ Combine water and butter in saucepan. Cook over medium heat until butter melts and mixture comes to a boil.
▶ Stir in flour all at once. Cook over low heat until mixture forms a ball, stirring constantly. Remove from heat.
▶ Add eggs 1 at a time, stirring vigorously with spoon until smooth and glossy after each addition.
▶ Drop dough by large spoonfuls onto ungreased baking sheet.
▶ Bake for 45 minutes or until puffed and golden. Cool. Cut tops off; remove soft centers. Fill with pudding, ice cream or fruit. Replace tops. Sprinkle confectioners' sugar on top.
▶ Yields 8 servings.

INDIVIDUAL CHOCOLATE SOUFFLÉS

4 eggs
⅓ cup milk
¼ cup sugar

8 ounces cream cheese,
softened
½ cup chocolate syrup

▶ Preheat oven to 375 degrees.
▶ Combine eggs, milk and sugar in blender container. Process mixture on low until blended. Add cream cheese gradually, processing until smooth.
▶ Add chocolate syrup. Blend for 10 seconds longer. Pour mixture into 4 1-cup soufflé dishes.
▶ Bake for 30 to 35 minutes or until custard is set. Serve immediately.
▶ Yields 4 servings.

All Things Being Equal

	When the recipe calls for:	You need:
BAKING	½ cup butter	1 stick
	2 cups butter	1 pound
	4 cups all-purpose flour	1 pound
	4½ to 5 cups sifted cake flour	1 pound
	1 square chocolate	1 ounce
	1 cup semisweet chocolate chips	1 6-ounce package
	4 cups marshmallows	1 pound
	2¼ cups packed brown sugar	1 pound
	4 cups confectioners' sugar	1 pound
	2 cups granulated sugar	1 pound
	4 cups Bisquick	1 pound
BREAD & CEREAL	1 cup fine dry bread crumbs	4 to 5 slices
	1 cup soft bread crumbs	2 slices
	1 cup small bread cubes	2 slices
	1 cup fine cracker crumbs	28 saltines
	1 cup fine graham cracker crumbs	15 crackers
	1 cup vanilla wafer crumbs	22 wafers
	1 cup crushed cornflakes	3 cups uncrushed
	4 cups cooked macaroni	1 8-ounce package
	3 cups cooked rice	1 cup uncooked
DAIRY	1 cup freshly grated cheese	¼ pound
	1 cup cottage cheese	1 8-ounce carton
	1 cup sour cream	1 8-ounce carton
	1 cup whipped cream	½ cup heavy cream
	⅔ cup evaporated milk	1 small can
	1⅔ cups evaporated milk	1 13-ounce can
FRUIT	4 cups sliced or chopped apples	4 medium
	1 cup mashed banana	3 medium
	2 cups pitted cherries	4 cups unpitted
	3 cups shredded coconut	½ pound
	4 cups cranberries	1 pound
	1 cup pitted dates	1 8-ounce package
	1 cup candied fruit	1 8-ounce package
	3 to 4 tablespoons lemon juice plus 1 teaspoon grated rind	1 lemon
	⅓ cup orange juice plus 2 teaspoons grated rind	1 orange
	4 cups sliced peaches	8 medium
	2 cups pitted prunes	1 12-ounce package
	2¾ cups raisins	1 15-ounce package

All Things Being Equal

	When the recipe calls for:	You need:
MEAT	4 cups chopped cooked chicken 2 cups chopped cooked meat 2 cups cooked ground meat	1 5-pound chicken 1 pound, cooked 1 pound, cooked
	1 cup chopped nuts	4 ounces, shelled 1 pound, unshelled
VEGETABLES	2 cups cooked green beans 2½ cups lima beans or red beans 4 cups shredded cabbage 1 cup grated carrots 1 4-ounce can mushrooms 1 cup chopped onion 4 cups sliced or chopped raw potatoes 2 cups canned tomatoes	½ pound fresh or 1 16-ounce can 1 cup dried, cooked 1 pound 1 large ½ pound, fresh 1 large 4 medium 1 16-ounce can

Common Equivalents

1 tablespoon = 3 teaspoons
2 tablespoons = 1 ounce
4 tablespoons = ¼ cup
5 tablespoons + 1 teaspoon
   = ⅓ cup
8 tablespoons = ½ cup
12 tablespoons = ¾ cup
16 tablespoons = 1 cup
1 cup = 8 ounces or ½ pint
4 cups = 1 quart
4 quarts = 1 gallon

6½ to 8-ounce can = 1 cup
10½ to 12-ounce can = 1¼ cups
14 to 16-ounce can (No. 300) = 1¾ cups
16 to 17-ounce can (No. 303) = 2 cups
1-pound 4-ounce can or 1-pint 2-ounce can
   (No. 2) = 2½ cups
1-pound 13-ounce can (No. 2½) = 3½ cups
3-pound 3-ounce can or 46-ounce can
   = 5¾ cups
6½-pound or 7-pound 5-ounce can (No. 10)
   = 12 to 13 cups

Metric Conversion Chart

Liquid

1 teaspoon	=	5 milliliters
1 tablespoon	=	15 milliliters
1 fluid ounce	=	30 milliliters
1 cup	=	250 milliliters
1 pint	=	500 milliliters

Dry

1 quart	=	1 liter
1 ounce	=	30 grams
1 pound	=	450 grams
2.2 pounds	=	1 kilogram

NOTE: The metric measures are approximate benchmarks for purposes of home food preparation.

What's In A Name?

AL DENTE—Italian term used to describe pasta that is cooked until slightly chewy.

BAKE—To cook food uncovered in an oven. When applied to meats and chicken, it is called roasting.

BARBECUE—To roast or broil food on a rack or spit over coals or under a heat unit. The food is frequently brushed with a sauce during cooking.

BASTE—To moisten food as it cooks to prevent the surface from drying out or to add flavor. Butter, drippings, fruit juices and sauces are generally used.

BEAT—To combine a mixture until smooth with rapid regular motion using a spoon, wire whisk or mixer.

BOIL—To cook food in liquid on the stove top.

BRAISE—To cook food over low heat in a small amount of liquid in a covered pan on the stove top. The food may be browned first in a small amount of oil.

BROTH—Liquid in which meat, poultry or vegetables have been simmered; same as stock.

BROWN—To fry food in a small amount of oil until the outside is brown.

CLOVE OF GARLIC—1 section of a garlic bulb.

COAT—To sprinkle food with or dip into flour or sauce until covered.

CREAM—To beat until smooth and blended, usually sugar with shortening.

CUT IN—To distribute shortening in flour or flour mixture by using pastry blender or 2 knives scissor-fashion until mixture resembles fine crumbs.

DASH—A very small amount, 1/8 teaspoon or less.

DRIPPINGS—Fat and juice released from meat or poultry during cooking.

FILET (or fillet)—A boneless piece of meat, fish or poultry.

FOLD IN—To combine delicate ingredients such as whipped cream or beaten egg whites with other ingredients using a gentle, circular cutting and lifting motion.

GARNISH—To add a decorative touch to food.

GLAZE—To coat with a glossy flavorful mixture.

GRILL—To cook food on a rack by direct heat, usually hot coals.

KNEAD—To work a food mixture, usually dough, with a pressing, folding motion to a well blended texture.

MARINADE—A seasoned liquid used to soak food, improve flavor and tenderize.

MARINATE—To soak in a marinade.

MERINGUE—Mixture of stiffly beaten egg whites and sugar, baked to a soft and lightly browned stage for desserts or cooked until crisp for dessert shells.

PAN-BROIL—To cook, uncovered, on the stove top over high heat on an ungreased or lightly greased hot surface, pouring off drippings as they accumulate.

PAN-FRY—To cook over high heat in small amount of shortening on stove top.

PREHEAT—To heat oven to desired temperature before baking.

PURÉE—To press food through a sieve or food mill, or to process in blender or food processor to a smooth consistency.

QUICHE—Main-dish pie made of eggs and cream in pie pastry. Vegetables, cheese, meat or poultry may be added.

ROAST—To cook meat or poultry uncovered in oven.

SAUTÉ—To cook lightly in oil or butter, stirring frequently.

SHRED—To cut food into thin slivers with knife or shredder.

SIMMER—To cook over low heat in liquid just below boiling point on stove top.

STEAM—To cook on a rack or in a colander over steaming hot water in a covered pan on stove top.

STEW—To cook food over low heat in a simmering liquid on the stove top.

STIR-FRY—To cook sliced or chopped food quickly in a small amount of oil in a skillet or wok, stirring constantly.

YEAST—Micro-organisms that produce carbon dioxide from carbohydrates that cause baked goods to rise to a light texture.

Index

160

Add To Your Cookbook Collection
or
Give As A Gift

FOR ORDERING INFORMATION

Favorite Recipes Press
a division of Great American Opportunities Inc.
P.O. Box 305142, Nashville, TN   37230
or
Call Toll-free
1-800-251-1542